THE WAY OF PRAYERFUL LIVING

everyday contemplative

L. ROGER OWENS

UPPER ROOM BOOKS®
NASHVILLE

Cover design and imagery: Jay and Kristi Smith at Juicebox Designs
Interior design and typesetting: PerfecType | Nashville, TN

Library of Congress Cataloging-in-Publication Data

Names: Owens, L. Roger, 1975- author.
Title: Everyday contemplative : the way of prayerful living / L. Roger Owens.
Description: Nashville, TN : Upper Room Books, [2022] | Includes bibliographical references. | Summary: "Roger Owens challenges readers to expand their definition of contemplative living to encompass all who seek to be more open, available, and responsive to God. Owens presents seven characteristics of contemplative living: longing, attention, patience, playfulness, vulnerability, nonjudgment, and freedom"-- Provided by publisher.
Identifiers: LCCN 2021051568 (print) | LCCN 2021051569 (ebook) | ISBN 9780835819916 (print) | ISBN 9780835819923 (epub)
Subjects: LCSH: Contemplation. | Prayer--Christianity. | Christian life.
Classification: LCC BV5091.C7 O94 2022 (print) | LCC BV5091.C7 (ebook) | DDC 248.3/4--dc23/eng/20211202
LC record available at https://lccn.loc.gov/2021051568
LC ebook record available at https://lccn.loc.gov/2021051569

For

Jill and David
with deepest love and gratitude

"I thank my God every time I remember you" (Phil. 1:3).

CONTENTS

ACKNOWLEDGMENTS

I began this book in January 2020, just as news of a novel coronavirus was spreading fear across the globe and in the United States. I am finishing the book in March 2021. Vaccines are beginning to offer a glimpse of hope, but fear of what the future holds still predominates. This is a pandemic book, yet rarely do I mention the pandemic itself. I have no doubt that the challenges of quarantine, fear, grief, and uncertainty have shaped these pages. Living radically open to God has never felt more necessary. Still, I don't believe living open to God in a pandemic is different in substance from living open to God in "normal" times. No doubt, the conditions of pandemic have sharpened my sense of what the substance of that kind of openness to God is. So I begin my thanks with gratitude for my family: my kids—Simeon, Silas, and Mary Clare—for all the walks, meals together, and conversations about what I'm writing. And for Ginger, for her love, patience, steadiness, and encouragement throughout these months and always. I'm grateful for Claire McKeever-Burgett and Johnny Sears, whose comments on a draft of the proposal for this book led me to make substantive changes. I'm grateful for the team at Upper Room Books, especially for Joanna Bradley Kennedy, who saw the potential in this book, and for Michael Stephens, who so thoughtfully edited each page. I'm also thankful for friends who read the manuscript and gave me invaluable feedback: Sr. Kathleen Flood, Abby Kocher, Craig Kocher, Ginger Thomas, Larry Williams, and Zelma Williams. I dedicate this book to my sister Jill and my brother David, whose love and encouragement have been a constant support.

An Invitation

> everyday *adj.* 1. Appropriate for ordinary days or routine occasions.
>
> 2. Commonplace; ordinary.

People who have read my other books on the spiritual life mention one character to me more than any other. Not my wife, who often strolls onto the page with a bemused smile and a wry comment. Not my children, who tumble into my books with their chaos, clever antics, and occasional bickering. And certainly not me.

No, more than any other, people mention a character that plays a key, literally supporting role: my green La-Z-Boy.

Because I write about prayer, I write about that chair, which I bought seventeen years ago and then heaved into the back of a station wagon. It entered our lives wrapped in cellophane and ready to perform its jobs, one of which is to be a place where I pray, where I sit and rest with God, where I seek to open my life to the divine love in which we live and move and have our being, though we are often unaware of that fact. It's where I try to notice and follow the threads of divinity woven through my life.

Just as often, of course, it's where I sit completely distracted, doing none of those things.

A few years ago, after frayed upholstery, a missing button, and coffee stains rendered the chair unfit for the family room, it was reassigned to the basement, where it greeted me most mornings, patiently waiting in a musty corner. A bookshelf stood to its left and a table—laden with a Bible, a candle, a journal, and, in the winter months, a sun-mimicking lamp—to its right. I would head to this chair before the rest of the house stirred, and I would pray.

Lately though, I've become increasingly aware of other roles that chair has played.

Over the past seventeen years, that chair has supported a lot more than my praying. I've also done a lot of living in that chair. How many hours have I spent rocking fussing babies, whining toddlers, and even disgruntled tweens in that chair! How many afternoons have I found a good nap in that chair! How many cups of coffee have I downed, snacks have I consumed, movies have I watched in that chair!

I've read and written books in that chair. I've eaten meals in that chair. I've participated in marital spats in that chair and uttered appropriate apologies in that chair.

I've played a game called "You'll Never Get Loose" countless times with my kids. My dad used to play it with my brother and me as he sat in his green La-Z-Boy, and now I sit in the chair, missing having kids small enough to play.

And from that chair, most mornings, I've been launched into the painfully beautiful, broken world where I live the rest of my life.

Sometimes I've been in that chair to pray. But more often, over the years, I've been there to live.

And the same divine love has surrounded me even then. Even then the same threads of divinity were weaving through my days.

The chair is becoming a symbol for me, a sign of what I long for more and more in my life with God: a unity between my praying and living. I want my praying to inform my living and my living to become a kind of prayer.

What would it look like to practice not just contemplative praying—set times of open, attentiveness to the Divine—but contemplative living? Can we—with or without a special green chair—live the minutes, hours, and days of our lives ever more attuned to those threads of divinity, ever more responsive to the pulsing rhythms of divine love that want to launch each one of us as a healing balm into a painfully beautiful, broken world?

Candidates for Contemplation?

Since I think of this book as an invitation, whose name should be on the front of the envelope?

The other day a friend from graduate school called my office. She is now a pastor in nearby West Virginia, but I hadn't seen her in years. She had a question she wanted to discuss and wondered if we could meet for lunch if she made the ninety-minute drive to the seminary where I teach.

She told me over the phone that she knows people who have spiritual directors—guides in the life of prayer and life with God—with whom they meet once a month or so to help them find their way through the darkness and confusion that life often is. I assume they had told her the benefits of having such a soul friend: the zone of nonjudgment they create; the way they have no agenda for your life; the value of knowing a holy chat is scheduled monthly; the sheer gift of having a place where you can laugh or cry, ponder or rage without fear; the little light their presence can cast into the dimness of your soul.[1] She'd started to wonder whether spiritual direction would be good for her, too.

"I'd like to talk to you about whether I might be a good candidate for spiritual direction," she said.

I agreed to chat over lunch. I looked forward to seeing an old friend. And the hands-down best Thai restaurant in Pittsburgh is just a mile away from the seminary. I love to take people there and recommend the pumpkin curry at a spice level not to exceed "four."

But it was winter, and she'd have a two-hour hilly drive and would need to check the forecast before embarking. So maybe I should have saved her the trouble of coming. Just knowing she was thinking about spiritual direction enough to wonder whether she was a good candidate, just by hearing how she had spoken with friends who were benefiting from this practice, and just by realizing she would be willing to brave the hills in the snow to have a conversation over an excellent curry dish, I had all the information I needed. "Yes," I should have told her. "You are a good candidate for spiritual direction."

Some folks might have the same question about contemplative praying and living: Am I a good candidate for *that*?

If there are any doubts, it's because we carry around in our minds stereotypical pictures of spiritual people, contemplative types who seem nothing like us: robed monks with sandaled feet and impossible haircuts who shuffle to prayer seven times a day, sometimes at hours when there's some question whether even God is awake. Desert hermits who live in caves and have friends deliver to them a loaf of crusty bread once a week to sustain them through their extreme ascetic practices, perhaps splurging on a plate of simple vegetables on feast days. Famous gurus who trumpet through their books, their podcasts, and their Twitter accounts that they are genuine mystics, lost in a profound oneness with the All.

No way am I a candidate for that kind of life, we think.

Or sometimes we read about contemplation, and it sounds so difficult, like a particular type of prayer that involves a lot of sitting and holding your hands just right and letting your vision go soft as you stare into a void—a kind of prayer you could only learn how to do if you signed up for a weeklong retreat, preferably at a facility on an idyllic island off the coast of the Washington State. (There are a lot of contemplatives in the Pacific Northwest, right?)

Odd people engaging in esoteric prayer on remote islands. *Thanks, but no thanks.*

But what if the word *contemplative* doesn't just name a narrowly defined kind of prayer—which it sometimes does—but also a possible approach to *all* prayer?

What if the same word doesn't denote a specific way of life—extreme, alone, with lots of somber sitting and eating simple vegetables—but can describe *any* life that seeks to be more open, available, and responsive to the One who is as present in an office cubicle as in a hermit's cell?

Sure, there are people living contemplatively in monasteries and convents (and people *not* living contemplatively there, too). There are also contemplatives working at library reference desks and delivering Amazon Prime packages, scrambling to complete tax returns in April and changing linens in hotel rooms. There are contemplatives talking about God from pulpits and contemplatives listening in the pews. And there are contemplatives in the colorful rooms beneath the sanctuary teaching the kids too young to endure preaching. Some of those kids are also contemplatives.

In other words, most contemplatives are *everyday* contemplatives. When I look up the word *everyday* in the dictionary, I see it means "common" and "ordinary."[2] Like faded blue jeans in the dresser drawer. Like you and me. Maybe our pictures should be in the dictionary next to the word.

Parents and principals can live contemplatively. Doctors and lawyers can be attentive to the Divine. Custodians and dentists can be open to God. Hospital orderlies and nursing home residents all have the capability of opening and responding to the refrains of divine love being sung from the depth of every soul.

Contemplatives are protesting with the Black Lives Matter movement. They are marching with the Poor People's Campaign. Contemplatives might start by sitting in a La-Z-Boy, but they don't stop there.

Perhaps some of these folks, if they've been allowing themselves to learn this refrain of Love over a long period of time, walk just a little slower, make eye contact a little more often, listen more patiently as you answer their question, "How are you?" They seem to show up in their lives and in your life as their authentic, truest selves. But they don't do so in a way that calls attention to themselves. More likely, it is in a way that gives greater attention to you.

And they almost never announce that they have become contemplatives.

Thomas Merton writes that contemplative praying and living is a "response to a call: a call from [God] Who has no voice, and yet Who speaks in everything that is, and Who, most of all, speaks in the depths of our own being: for we ourselves are words of [God]."[3]

To live contemplatively means simply to approach life with openness, availability, and growing responsiveness to the God who speaks in everything, to the God who speaks from the depths of our very selves, to the God who spoke us into existence.

If you were to Google the seminary where I teach, find my office phone number on the faculty page, and ring me to ask whether you're a good candidate to be an everyday contemplative, I'd say three things.

First, I'd say, "Please call me 'Roger.'"

Second, I'd ask, "How far away do you live, and what's your opinion of pumpkin curry?"

Finally, I'd answer your question: "Yes, of course you are."

Approaching This Book

This book is not a "how-to." I will not offer seven sure-fire steps to contemplative bliss. If I could, I'd be the guru with bestselling books, a podcast, and a hundred thousand Twitter followers.

But I can't because those steps don't exist.

This book is an invitation to approach prayer and life differently, with a posture of receptivity that allows you to become ever more open, available, and responsive to the recreating work of God's Spirit in your life and in the world. It's an invitation to a paradigm shift, an exploration of an alternative way and of what that way can look like in the rough-and-tumble of actual existence.

A few years ago, I wrote a book called *What We Need Is Here: Practicing the Heart of Christian Spirituality*.[4] That book introduced readers to several spiritual practices—ways of prayer—through which God gives Godself to us, and it taught specific practices like sitting with God in silence, praying the Psalms, and contemplating the Gospels. I consider this book a sort of prequel to that one. If that book introduced particular practices, this one explores a contemplative approach you can take to *all* spiritual practices— indeed, to life itself.

Or as I say in the first chapter, this book is an invitation to spirituality in the passive voice. That chapter puts some more flesh on what I mean by contemplative praying and living. It lays the foundation for the seven chapters that follow, each one exploring a particular characteristic of a contemplative approach to praying and living. Those characteristics are as follows:

- Longing
- Attention
- Patience
- Playfulness
- Vulnerability
- Nonjudgment
- Freedom

Some of these characteristics are so closely related and interdependent that I sometimes wonder if the list should only have five or six. At other times, I think maybe I should add a couple more. Or several more. I don't intend this list to be definitive or exhaustive but suggestive, just enough to get you following more closely the lead of your divine Dance Partner.

This book is an invitation to consider a new perspective on life and prayer, one that counters the just-get-on-with-it, make-something-happen impulse of our culture. I hope these chapters will give you something to think about, so, along the way, you'll notice questions in the margins labeled "Consider This." These are meant to spur further thinking about the ideas in each chapter and how they relate to your life.

But we can't just think ourselves into a life of openness to God. Living as an everyday contemplative is not an affair of the mind alone; it's only available to us in practice. That's why the margins also have "Try This" suggestions, invitations to try this approach to praying and living in the messiness and ambiguity of real life.

At the end of each chapter, I've provided spiritual exercises, ways to take the ideas and themes of the chapter and let them inform specific times of prayer—periods of twenty to thirty minutes (no green chair required) of doing nothing but giving your fullest attention to God, saying, "Here I am God, open, available, and ready to respond. And here you are as well, I trust. How wonderful for us both!"

I've recently been listening to a podcast called *The Happiness Lab* to endure my forty-five-minute treadmill sessions at the gym. Each episode explores one shift we can make in our lives that will contribute to growth in happiness and overall well-being. A recent episode suggested that sharing an activity with others increases our enjoyment of that activity. That's why, when you're watching a movie with your teenage sons (hypothetically speaking, of course) and they text their friends the whole time, you enjoy the experience less because the movie watching isn't truly shared. The podcast described an experiment that showed that people enjoyed tasting chocolate more when someone else was tasting with them.[5]

Since I want you to enjoy reading this book and to grow in your enjoyment of life with God, I suggest you journey through these pages with others. I suspect you'll get more out of the "Consider This" questions when they become prompts for conversation. You'll appreciate the "Try This" suggestions and spiritual exercises more when you have a group of fellow pilgrims with whom to share your experiences.

A contemplative life—a fully human life open to God—was never meant to be lived alone. Why not live it with others, discovering with your companions what attentiveness, patience, playfulness, and the other characteristics of an everyday contemplative approach to life look like in community?

An Invitation

If I knew your name, I'd have my son who practices beautiful handlettering write it on an envelope so you'd know for sure that this invitation to approach prayer and life differently is addressed to you.

I recently remembered another name I need him to write on an envelope: my own. I still need the invitation to become more open, available, and responsive to the Holy Spirit's presence in my life.

A few mornings ago, I went to Panera Bread to work on this book. It's harder for me these days to write in the mornings in my green La-Z-Boy (it's hard for me to pray there these days, too). With high-schoolers in the house, everyone is up so much earlier, so my early morning alone-time has disappeared. We also added a wall in the basement and turned the room where I used to write and pray into a bedroom so my two growing sons could have spaces of their own. Now my desk and chair sit in what is essentially a hallway in the basement, through which the son who sleeps downstairs traipses back and forth from his bedroom to the bathroom every morning. Such traffic is not conducive to concentration. But Panera Bread has proven a hospitable place for early morning scribbling.

I'd just dropped the boys off at school and pulled into the parking lot around 7:30 on a Friday morning. I had come here to steal time to write, since I was nearing the end of a six-month stint as an acting dean and vice president at the seminary. I thought the work of being a dean would wind down in the last weeks before the return of the real dean, but I found myself completely thrown off course by well-laid plans falling through, conflicts requiring mediation, and student issues that could not wait. My anxiety, which is often high and which had been even higher during my six-month sojourn in the land of academic administration, had been spiking that week. I'd become breathless, careening from one meeting to another and replying to countless emails in between. But no one would find me at Panera.

I stepped out of my car, swung open the door to the back seat to grab my notebook and a pen, and hurried toward the restaurant, where a cup of caffeine would push my nervous system even closer to the edge.

Then, out of the corner of my eye, I glimpsed pink in the sky. I took two more steps in the direction of Panera; then I paused and turned. It was late January. The days had only been getting longer for a month. January is one of the cloudiest months in Pittsburgh, which is one of the cloudiest cities in the country. The chances of seeing a pastel sunrise were slim. You'd have to be at the right place at the right time—and I was.

I halted my march toward my day's first cup of coffee and gave my attention to the gift of beauty in the eastern sky, orange-blending-into-pink reflecting off the underside of cirrus clouds: a feast for the eyes. And to think I'd almost missed it.

The Song of Zechariah from the Gospel of Luke came to my mind: "By the tender mercy of our God, the dawn from on high will break upon us, to give light to those who sit in darkness" (1:78-79). Seeing dawn from on high is rare in a Pittsburgh winter, but the divine dawning of grace never ends. Had I been missing that, too?

And I thought of Merton. What if the divine voice really does speak to us through everything that is? What if this brief bit of nature's art really was a gift of God's grace, an untranslatable but no less enjoyable Word of the Lord spoken in silence, spoken in love? What if I had missed it?

And how many times over the past six months had I missed that voice speaking to me, wooing me and warning me—both through the world around me and from the depth of my own being—because I'd forgotten about approaching life differently? I'd been so busy making things happen, I'd resisted allowing Another to make things happen in me.

I need the invitation as badly as anyone. I don't write this book from the perspective of expertise or mastery—what is mastery in the spiritual life anyway? I write as a companion on the way, as one who has smelled the possibility of living open to God and has followed the scent far enough to be able to describe the smell. But I also know there is a meal waiting, and I realize what I'm really doing is writing my way to the banquet table where God longs to break bread with us, to share this life with us, and to be our most intimate companion.

I guess the real invitation is for both of us to journey toward the feast together. An everyday feast for everyday contemplatives.

1

Practicing Spirituality in the Passive Voice

Posture

[Y]ou put us on your way, bringing comfort and saying: "Run, I will carry you, and I will see you through to the end, and there I will carry you."

—St. Augustine, *The Confessions*, VI

W hen I was still a pastor, I mentioned in a sermon that I'm not good at getting things started—or finished. My leadership strengths are in the area one author calls "ideation." A less generous author would have called it the strength of idle daydreaming.

This confession likely came as no surprise to anyone who'd been in my office and read the titles of some of my books: *Making Ideas Happen*; *Getting Things Done*; *To Do, Doing, Done!*

After worship that day, Jack called the parsonage. Jack is an entrepreneur; he specializes in making things happen. "Roger, are you going to be around in a few minutes?" he asked. "I have a book I want to bring you." I don't often turn down a free book.

Twenty minutes later, Jack stood at the door holding a book called *In Search of Excellence: Lessons from America's Best-Run Companies.*

"It's a classic business book," he said. "You might want to skip straight to chapter 5."

As we chatted in the driveway where my children were drawing with sidewalk chalk, I tried to play the interested host, but I was thinking the whole time, *I wish he'd leave so I could see what's so special about chapter 5.*

When he left, I flipped to the table of contents and found the title of the fifth chapter: "A Bias for Action."[1]

Jack was offering me not-so-subtle leadership advice: Stop sitting, cease planning, and get on with it!

There are situations in which this is wise counsel for leaders because the "thinking up" needs to stop, and the action needs to start. When the need to get a plan just right becomes paralyzing, Jack's advice can be good.

But you need only to survey the wider cultural landscape or the landscape of many congregations (or perhaps the landscape of your own life?) to see that we live in a pervasively biased-for-action culture. If we're not starting something, doing something, trying something, or growing something, we might as well not exist. Our value is often measured by our utility, our capacity to accomplish goals. When we evaluate our leadership, physical health, or relationships, we feel compelled to meet a goal or secure an outcome—to make something happen.

> **CONSIDER THIS:**
> How do you see a bias for action at work in your culture? the church? your own life?

That same bias for action can slip into our life with God and infect our spiritual life. We forget that we are not the only agent in our life; there is another loving Agent acting within and about us, inviting us to respond. We have forgotten, if we ever knew, Quaker mystic Thomas R. Kelly's wisdom that "all our apparent initiative is already a response, a testimonial to [God's] secret presence and working within us."[2]

Since our spiritual life isn't just a slice of our life but our whole life seen from the perspective of relationship with God, what happens when we forget to surrender to the presence and agency of the living Christ within us, the very Life within our life? Here's what: We burn ourselves out making things happen.

The apostle Paul writes in the letter to the Philippians that we should "work out [our] salvation with fear and trembling; for it is God who is at work in [us], enabling [us] both to will and to work for his good pleasure" (2:12-13). *Salvation* here doesn't mean going to heaven alone but realizing our full flourishing in life with God both now and in eternity.

As a professor of Christian spirituality and a retreat leader, I see a lot of folks, many of them young people preparing to be pastors, who emphasize in their lives the "work out your own" aspect of these verses, strategizing prayer and life with God. They are ambitious to make something happen. They are finally going to pray themselves into a life that pleases God, hoping that God will respond.

It's hard to imagine it any other way. It's difficult to conceive of a divine Agent within us, working more deeply and profoundly than we ourselves are able, a holy Love that is already pleased with us and wants to liberate us for a life that is open, available, and responsive to that Love.

It's hard to imagine a way of praying and living that doesn't seize the reins of initiative but instead responds to God's initiative.

Spirituality in the Passive Voice

I should know. I was one of those ambitious young people, ready to change the world with my praying.

At least for a couple of weeks.

The first book I ever read on prayer was *The Hour That Changes the World: A Practical Plan for Personal Prayer.*[3] I was still relatively new in my Christian convictions, my heart still warmed by the heat of my faith's early zeal. As a first-year college student, I was ready to prove my Christian credentials. Bolstered by the attention and praise I'd received as a teenager for my newfound faith, I entered college determined to excel at the endeavor of faith. All I needed was the perfect plan to give shape to my ambition. That's when I came across *The Hour That Changes the World.*

The author, Dick Eastman, places the responsibility of prayer squarely in our hands. The world needs us to pray. God needs us to pray. He quotes approvingly the nineteenth-century preacher Charles Spurgeon, who said, "Prayer is the slender nerve that moveth the muscles of omnipotence."[4]

Eastman divides the hour of prayer into twelve different categories, ensuring that the hour covers every kind of prayer he could find in scripture, including acts of praise, confession, intercession, and singing. If the one praying would give five minutes to each kind of prayer, the power of God would be unleashed in the world. Eastman writes, "To be effective our sixty minutes with God should be carefully arranged. Systematic prayer adds health to the devotional habit. It helps us get started and keeps us going. . . . In fact, without a systematic approach to life, many goals would remain unreached." He continues, "The same is true with prayer. The devotional exercise needs careful planning and preparation to function properly."[5] It's as if God were waiting for us to read Eastman's book and get down to business so that God could finally do something.

It never occurred to me to question that careful planning and having a foolproof system could make my prayer "effective"; that prayer was akin to other activities in life, having a "goal" it was up to me to reach; that my "exercise" of prayer would only "function properly" if *I* performed it right.

I just started. I listed the twelve kinds of prayer in my journal each day while my roommate was in class, and I proceeded to change the world.

For a handful of days, that is, until I couldn't anymore.

Maybe it was the new freedom of college that got in my way—the freedom to waste time and sleep at odd hours, the freedom to make late night trips to Perkins to drink coffee and pretend to study or to Steak-N-Shake to drink milkshakes and not even pretend to study, the freedom to order pizza at midnight as a prelude to the studying that still needed to be done, a freedom that militates against a systematic, regimented approach to prayer.

But it is more likely my *approach* to prayer itself got in the way. My prayer was all about *me*: my work, my faith, my initiative. And my soul simply couldn't sustain such an exercise. Changing the world through prayer wears you out even if you don't down a whole pizza in the middle of the night.

> **CONSIDER THIS:**
> Recall your earliest experience with prayer. How would you describe your approach to prayer then? How has your approach changed since then?

I still needed to learn the wisdom of Julian of Norwich, who saw that "our Lord is the foundation from which our prayers arise" and that prayer "is given to us by the grace of his love."[6]

I still needed to learn the wisdom of popular Quaker author Richard Foster, who writes, "By themselves the Spiritual Disciplines can do nothing; they can only get us to the place where something can be done. . . . [They are] the means by which we place ourselves where [God] can bless us."[7]

> **TRY THIS:** Write a poem or a page in your journal, entitled "My History with Prayer." Reread what you have written. What sticks out to you? Surprises you?

The place where something *can be done.*

I still needed to discover spirituality in the passive voice.

The Lesson of the Fig Tree

In other words, I needed to learn the lesson of the fig tree.

Jesus tells a story about a man who owned a vineyard and had a fig tree planted in it (see Luke 13:6-9). But the tree didn't produce any fruit. Year after year he looked forward to canned figs and fig jelly and fig pie and fresh figs and figgy pudding, and year after year he found the tree barren. Tired of this annual disappointment, he told the gardener, "I'm done with it. Cut the thing down."

But the gardener urged patience. "Give me some time," he said. He proposed a remedy: He would loosen the soil around the base of the tree and put fertilizer on it to see if next year the tree would bear fruit.

One of the easiest ways to kill a tree is by compacting the soil. Ideal soil, according to an article I found, should be 50 percent porous space so it can hold water and oxygen for the roots. When the soil is compacted, the roots become suffocated and dehydrated.[8] So it makes sense that the gardener loosened the soil from around suffocated, dehydrated roots and then applied fertilizer. Roots cut off from the sources of life—air and water—can't nourish a tree.

> **CONSIDER THIS:**
> How do the roots of your life feel right now? Compressed? Dehydrated? Healthy? What are they crying out for?

Sometimes when people begin to feel drawn to prayer, when they sense a longing welling up inside of them for a life with God, they express that longing this way: *I feel cut off from the source of life! My roots are starving for air and can't breathe!*

26

We notice a longing, a desire, a thirst, inchoate at first, to stretch out to God the source of Life, to have a deep, conscious connection with the Divine, and so we ask: *How should I pray? How can I live a life with God?*

If we're good modern, success-oriented people, raised in a bias-for-action culture, we might think: *What do* I *need to do? How do* I *get on with it?* I *must take initiative!*

But the roots have no air or water. There's nothing these roots can do to change the situation. This was clear to the vineyard owner: From the outside, the tree looked dead, of no use except for firewood come winter.

But the gardener knew better.

The gardener knew that even if the roots couldn't take the initiative and change their own situation, he could. He could loosen the soil. He could add fertilizer. He could get things started. He could put the roots back in touch with the source of life. Christians have a name for this work of the divine Gardener on our behalf: *grace.*

Ruth Burrows, a Carmelite sister in England, has devoted most of the nine decades of her life to prayer, and she has learned something. "Prayer," she writes, "is not *our* activity, *our* getting in touch with God, *our* coming to grips with or making ourselves desirable to God. We can do none of these things, nor do we need to, for God is there, ready to do everything for us, loving us unconditionally."[9]

> **CONSIDER THIS:** How do you react to the notion that prayer is not primarily our activity?

When we notice that longing, that desire to connect with Life, that yearning to live contemplatively, and when we find ourselves wanting to grow in prayer and live fully in touch with God, that means the divine Gardener is digging, loosening the soil. God is already there doing what needs to be done.

Instead of seizing the initiative in our life with God (which, remember, is our *whole* life), the first thing to do is simply realize that Someone is sneaking into the shed and getting the shovel. Someone is loosening the soil so that our roots can breathe. Someone is already applying life-giving nutrients.

And when we hear that shovel hitting the dirt, the scratch of metal against the hard soil, it's not we who wield the shovel but God.

Living as an everyday contemplative begins with this realization: God is already at work; the initiative is God's.

> **TRY THIS:** Make a list of key moments in your life when you were aware that God was at work. How did you know? How did that feel? Do you sense that one of those moments is now?

A New Approach, a Different Posture

You likely wouldn't be reading this book if you hadn't already recognized that longing (more on longing in the next chapter), if you hadn't noticed in your spirit a desire to move from being the one in charge of praying and living to being open, available, and responsive to the God who is the foundation and source of our prayer and our life.

You want to pray and live contemplatively.

But how do we go against the grain of our culture? How do we approach praying and living *differently*?

One of the mistakes I made as a teenager was to umpire Little League Baseball. I must have been desperate for an extra fifteen bucks every week and a free slushy. Why else would I have opened myself to the ire of impassioned parents, the insults of disrespectful players, and the intimidation tactics of volunteer coaches?

My umpiring tenure was only slightly more successful than my earlier career as a player: two years on the worst team in the league. Over those years, I managed to make contact with the ball only once—a foul tip on my very last at bat. But my on-base percentage was pretty good, since I would rarely swing at the ball. Fourth grade pitchers aren't known for their accuracy, so my chances of getting a walk or being hit by a pitch were favorable.

I'm an observer by nature. My years on the baseball field as a player and an umpire afforded me the opportunity to see how different players approach the game. The weakest players are exiled to left field, where their presence does the least damage (I know—I spent some time out there myself). Since the ball so rarely makes it to left field, these kids exude boredom. They pay attention to everything but the game. They watch the moths fly around the outfield lights. They pick their noses. They wave at their parents in the stands, who mouth exaggeratedly, "You're doing great!" When the rare line drive sails between the shortstop and third baseman, the left fielder doesn't have a clue until the ball has whizzed past him. Only then does he chase the ball as it rolls toward the fence.

He's not standing on the balls of his feet, not holding his glove at ready, not watching the game. His posture says much about his approach and readiness for the sport of baseball.

During the years I was a player and an umpire, I also avidly cheered for the Chicago Cubs. For some reason now lost to me, I aspired to be a catcher. I idolized Jody Davis, catcher for the Cubs in the mid-1980s. I'd squat in the backyard like Jody Davis, catcher's mitt positioned in front of me, while my friend Chris hurled pitches in my direction.

Jody Davis's posture said something completely different about his approach to the game. He crouched down, balanced on the balls of his feet, one arm held behind his back. He had to be alert, ready to tear off his mask and run in any direction: down the third-base line to chase a bunt, toward a dugout to catch a pop fly, backward to retrieve a wild pitch. He had to always know the situation on the field, always be ready to throw out a potential base-stealer.

His posture radiated alertness. It said something about his approach to and readiness for the game, something very different from a distracted Little League left fielder's.

For both the unfortunate left fielder and the professional catcher, their postures were literally how they held and carried their bodies. They also had inner postures, attitudes, and perspectives that shaped their readiness.

If we expand our use of the word *posture* from the merely physical to metaphorical, then we can use it to describe our approach to any activity or endeavor.

Even the activity of prayer. Even the endeavor of living. Even being an everyday contemplative.

I've been wondering over the last few years about an appropriate posture for a contemplative approach to praying and living, to an integrated life with God, a posture that benches its bias for action and sidelines rugged self-sufficiency and the ego's determination to make something happen. What would a posture look like that allows for a spirituality in the passive voice and puts the agency of God on center stage? How might we imagine a life posture that honors God's initiative and seeks to be increasingly open, available, and responsive to the transforming work of God's Spirit in our lives and in the world?

> **TRY THIS:** Pretend (when no one is watching) you are a baseball player, and practice different postures. Practice being bored and distracted then alert and attentive. How does that feel? Which posture feels like a metaphor for your life with God right now?

What might a posture be in the spiritual life that "gets us to the place where something can be done," as Richard Foster put it?

The next seven chapters consider characteristics of just such a posture.

Taken

But first, one more image.

One of the great gifts of the pastoral life is to baptize babies. Performing these baptisms is one of the things I miss most about being a pastor. Now, whenever I witness an infant baptism, that second birth in the Spirit, I can't help but remember that the child was born first in a hospital a few months earlier. If the baby cries when it's baptized, it's a good thing it can't remember the travail of birth. After all, for the nine months of gestation, the child enjoyed a warm bath, muted light, and the calming rhythm of the mother's heartbeat—basically a spa. Then suddenly—or what must seem suddenly to the child, if not to the mother—that's gone. The lights are bright, the air is cold, and the mother's steady heartbeat has vanished: The baby is born.

So what does that newborn do?

The child cries. Those legs and arms tense up, the fists clench, and the child wails. She's working hard. She had no idea she possessed the capacity for this kind of exertion. She's whisked away by a nurse and is measured and poked and wiped, all the while still wailing. Then, if everything is going well (I've been in the delivery room when it didn't), someone—a midwife, a nurse, a partner—carries the child back to the mother and places her on Mom's chest. And it's warm again. And it's quiet again. And there's that heartbeat again. And the baby calms down because she's home, right where she knows she belongs.

At this point, the baby's thinking: *It worked! All that crying and scream-ing, all the wriggling and wailing—it worked. It got me back where I belong. Back to the heartbeat of love. Back home. I'm going to do this the rest of my life!*

But we know better, don't we? She had to be *taken*. Lifted and carried. There was no other way.

Our truest home is next to the heartbeat of God. Not only in some distant heavenly future but right now. Our truest home is listening and responding to God's heartbeat of love for us and for the world. But that's not a destination we can choose and then assuredly plot our course to by adopting practices of prayer and ways of living that will propel us to our destination. As soon as it becomes a destination that we're determined to reach by our own effort and ingenuity—our own bias for action—we're headed in the wrong direction.

But we can be taken. We can be loved into that place. We can be lifted and carried. And the greatest challenge of the spiritual life is to allow ourselves to be taken, to allow ourselves to be loved all the way to our truest home.

Spiritual Exercises

Sacred Reading

Philippians 2:1-13; Galatians 5:22-26.
(See directions for sacred reading on page 155.)

Practicing Awareness

Take fifteen minutes and, in a spirit of prayer and with an attitude of open-ness to God, use these questions to look over yesterday or last week:

- When did I notice God at work or taking initiative in my life during this period? How did that feel?
- When during this period was I struggling to seize control of my life or make something happen? How did that feel?
- When have I been able to surrender to what God was doing in my life?
- How have my actions or attitudes stood in the way of God's work in my life?
- What am I learning about how I want to *be* with God from what I am noticing in this time of self-examination?

Close with a prayer, giving thanks for what God has shown you and asking God to help you to be more aware of and responsive to God's loving agency in your life.

Prompts for Journaling

Write a letter to God about how you have approached prayer in your life and naming any confusions you have about how God has been at work in your praying and your living. Be honest. Let God know how you *want* to be open to God's Spirit carrying you to your truest home in God.

Now, write a letter to yourself *from* God. How do you imagine God would respond to the letter you wrote to God?

2

Following Our
Ultimate Desire

Longing

The most typical evidence of grace being at work in us is
not that we find ourselves aware of a duty, but that we find
ourselves aware of a desire.

—SIMON TUGWELL, OP

I was up at 5:30 a.m. to practice my sermon one Sunday morning—the
curse of agreeing to preach at a church with an 8:00 a.m. service. Fortunately, the church was only one mile from my home, or I would have had
to set my alarm even earlier.

At that hour of the day, I have several longings: to be back in bed, to
take a hot shower, to drink a gallon of coffee.

For the sun to already be shining.

For the church to call me and tell me they've canceled worship for the
day. One can always hope, right?

On this morning, I was pacing around the family room committing
my sermon to memory when I looked out the front door and saw a family of
deer enjoying a satisfying breakfast in my front lawn, five in all, their long

necks bent toward the grass, their mouths silently chomping whatever sustenance the lawn offered. Otherwise, they looked like statues—so silent, so still, not spooked by my presence at the glass door. In the moment, I wondered if these were the deer of Psalm 42, longing for the gentle ripples of a stream, longing for the refreshment of clean, clear water. "As the deer longs for flowing streams," the palmist writes, "so my soul longs for you, O God" (v. 1).

That pause at the door became an opportunity for brief self-examination. Beneath all the other early morning wants, what do I truly long for? Do I long for God as these deer long to be fed and refreshed?

I began to think about the folks whose alarms would be beeping in an hour or so, who would roll out of their beds and shower and dress in their Sunday best and drain a mug of coffee, scarf down breakfast, and head off to worship: *What longing will pull them to the house of the Lord? Will I be preaching to people who are longing for God, who are longing for a word from the Lord, who are longing to fulfill their human purpose in praise to God? What longings impel them?*

I'd preached at this church enough that I could imagine those early-service worshipers. Some I knew by name. While I didn't know the immediate reason any of them was going to church that morning—a chance to see and be seen, a sense of guilt or duty, desire to please a spouse, love of music, a genuine longing for God—I did know what was ultimately drawing them to worship.

I could stand before the fifty or so people gathered in the small chapel, look them in the eye, and know exactly what they want. I would be addressing people who are like deer, who are longing desperately to sip from the gentle brooks of God's grace. Some of them just need to discover this for themselves.

I know they want God, whether *they* know it or not.

A Complicated Longing

I didn't know this about these people because I possess psychic powers. I know they long for God because that is what the Christian spiritual traditions teach about what it means to be human.

As soon as we step into the territory of human longing, and especially of thinking and talking about the most fundamental longings that make us who we are, we have entered what theologians call *theological anthropology*: Christian thinking about what it means to be human. And there are two basic premises of theological anthropology that allow me to know something about every human being I meet—every person I pass on my evening walk, every kid crowding against me at a Chinese buffet, and every soul brave enough to show up early on a Sunday morning to worship.

Premise #1: Human beings have a built-in longing for God. We naturally pine for the supernatural. We desire God, and that desire is part of what makes us human.

This longing for God mirrors God's own longing for us. In the story of Creation in Genesis, we learn that God created human beings in God's own image. On this marvelous globe, full—at one time or another—of velociraptors, six-ton ground sloths, saber-toothed tigers, King Charles Spaniels, kestrels and the mice they eat, dandelions and lilacs and giant sequoias, God wanted a creature that could reflect God's own being: God's love and mercy, God's mind and heart, God's delight in the rest of creation. God longed for a creature that could self-consciously return God's love and longing. So God made human beings in God's own image. That's something of what it means to be made in God's image—to naturally be able to reciprocate God's own longing for us. In the case of the divine image, like seeks like. We are like God; we long for God.

It's completely natural.

Premise #2: The built-in human longing for God gets twisted into a longing for things that are not God. Sometimes when Christianity talks about sin, this confused longing is what is meant. And it's completely *unnatural*.

"Sin" is the name we give for the reality that, though deep down we long for intimacy with God, we have become oblivious to the true nature of our longing (indeed, to the true nature of our very selves) and we, as they say, settle. We settle for things we can see, touch, and taste. We settle, hoping these things will satisfy and calm our inherent restlessness. It's not wrong to enjoy the good things of life (a splash of almond extract in my coffee in the morning! a piece of dark chocolate after dinner!), but we must not expect them to do a job they can't—fulfill our longing to enjoy the love of God. We ask too much of them.

The truth is we'll never be satisfied.

The name for the reality that we'll never be satisfied is "hedonic adaptation." That's a fancy way to say that we get used to pleasurable things. We adapt to them so that eventually they fail to give us the pleasure they once gave, and then we want more. Marketers are acutely aware of this psychological phenomenon. They know that the new phone you just bought, with more bells and whistles than you could possibly ever use

> **CONSIDER THIS:** How does this understanding of what sin is—seeking to fulfill our longing for God through other things—relate to how you have thought about sin? How does this new understanding make any difference in your life?

> **TRY THIS:** Make a list of the things you are longing for in your life right now. Which of these things do you think can bring ultimate satisfaction?

(*But have you seen how wonderful the camera is on this phone?!!*) will make you sublimely happy until the aura of its newness wears off in about three months, at which point there will be a newer model promising even more sublime happiness (*But have you seen how much better the camera is on the latest model?!!*) if you'd only buy it. *Ad infinitum.*

We'll never be satisfied.

My family likes to go to the beach in North Carolina. One of our favorite beaches to visit is called Carolina Beach. We love Carolina Beach for one reason: Britt's Donut Shop. When we get within a hundred miles of the beach, a craving strikes us all. This is not one of those new gourmet donut shops where you can get crème brûlée donuts, maple bacon donuts, or Gorgonzola pistachio donuts (okay, I made that one up). No, Britt's makes one donut: a simple yeast donut. And they make them all day long. My stomach growls at just the thought. The children go crazy at the word *Britt's.* When we get to the beach, we park and make our way to Britt's, just off the boardwalk. Each donut costs a dollar; each person gets two donuts. We pay for our donuts then sit down on a bench outside the store, each of us with a small bag containing two rings of sugary happiness. Ten seconds later . . . it's over. They are gone, and we are left with the desire for more and a sugar crash in about an hour. They satisfied us. Briefly.

That story shows what it feels like to set our sights too low, hoping that the glittering people and objects that populate our lives will somehow quench the deepest thirst of our souls and settle our stubborn restlessness. After the phone, after the donut, after the car, after the relationship, we keep asking, "Isn't there more?"

We ask because the answer is yes.

Awakening to Our Longing

Rarely does that natural, in-built desire for God appear obvious at first. Longing for God is not like seeing an old college friend after many years in an unlikely place and recognizing her instantly. "Sally, so good to see you! You haven't changed a bit!" Rather, longing for God sneaks up on you, sometimes in disguise.

The work of God's grace begins to wake us up so we can notice that our longings are scattered in all kinds of zigging and zagging directions, and we realize our job, house, or partner will not ultimately satisfy. (What a relief that realization must be to the partner; how it takes the pressure off to be freed of that burden!) So we begin to ask ourselves, *What's this longing business all about?* If, as James K. Smith says in his book on the spirituality of St. Augustine, "the terrain of our interior life is a wilderness of wants,"[1] then what do we really want? I mean, *really*.

I remember how longing for God began to appear to me at first. I was an anxious, stressed high school student, and I started going to church with my girlfriend some Sunday mornings and most Sunday nights. I'd never been to a church where people seemed so eager to be there, where adults brought their Bibles and sat through in-depth Bible studies, taking notes on the very pages of holy writ. I'd never seen people walk to the front of a sanctuary during worship to give a testimony, to speak honestly about what God was doing in their lives. (I don't think I'd ever heard someone other than a preacher or a Sunday school teacher talk about God at all.) I marveled at how the whole congregation sang the hymns joyously in four-part harmony. And people came back to church *again* in the evening—I was incredulous. Amid these outward manifestations of their faith pulsed a spiritual energy, something I didn't have words for. But I wanted to know what it was.

I followed that longing. And as I followed it, it led me to a deeper place within myself that I wasn't yet ready to recognize; I sensed a lack, a void, and suspected that whatever it was that gave these people joy might fill that lack.

That's how it started for me. But the longing for God can appear to us in a number of forms, shrouded in the desires that begin to surface when our superficial lives start to feel too shallow. It can begin as . . .

. . . a desire to belong, to feel more deeply at home in our families and communities, more deeply at home on this planet.

. . . a hunger for purpose and meaning, for a sense that our life matters.

. . . a pull to fight injustice in our neighborhoods, institutions, and world.

. . . a longing for wholeness and peace, for a life that doesn't seem fractured and dissipated.

. . . a draw toward more true beauty in our lives.

As Quaker minister and writer J. Brent Bill reminds us, "Our souls hunger for beauty wherever they can find it. They do so because our hunger for beauty is a hunger for God, whether we're aware of it or not. We yearn in the deepest part of ourselves for real and profound connection to the divine."[2]

> **CONSIDER THIS:**
> When have you sensed a longing for God through something on this list? What kind of longings would you add to the list?

It was more than half my life ago that I began to recognize a longing for God, even if I didn't name it that at the time. Since then that longing has taken other forms as well: a longing to offer myself more deeply to others in love; a sense of wonder at the mystery of all that is; an ability to be touched by the sight of true beauty, self-sacrifice, and love in action. Whenever one of these feelings arises in me, I can greet it as one of the ways that yearning for a "profound connection to the divine" makes itself known in me.

> **CONSIDER THIS:** How did you first recognize a longing for God in your life? How does that longing continue to show up in your life?

But I've also endured desert seasons when my longing for God has seemingly withered. In those periods—sometimes called dark nights of the soul—God is often leading us to desire God for God's own sake and not simply for the good feelings that can come from a relationship with God. As painful as such seasons of the soul can be, I recognized during them that I still had at least a desire to desire God again; my longing for God took that meager form—and it was enough.

However the desire for God begins to show up in our lives, we can trust that God's grace is at work, that a divine love is active in us, waking us up to the deepest—often hidden—reason for our very existence and freeing us to begin to follow that longing to its truest end: friendship with God, genuine enjoyment of the One who made us.

So What Do I Do Now?

Here's a thought experiment. Suppose that the sermon I was rehearsing as I gazed at the deer through our front door was on Psalm 42, a sermon about human longing for God. Further, suppose that when I preached it three hours later to fifty early-rising Presbyterians, I suggested that longing for God—which is quite natural—is an aspect of a posture toward praying and living that can help us remain open, available, and responsive to the trans-forming work of God's Spirit in our lives. And imagine that several con-gregants approached me after the service because they were so enthralled by what I had said that they wanted to hear more (simultaneously every preacher's dream and worst nightmare). Specifically, they wondered what they should do if they wanted to have such a robust longing for God in their own lives—they wanted to be like those deer—but didn't recognize that longing. "I don't know if I long for God or not," one of them said. "What do I do?"

Here's the first thing I'd say: Whatever you do, don't try to manufac-ture a longing. Don't leave thinking you heard that you "should" long for God, and then try harder. A longing for God is not something you can produce; there's no instructional YouTube video to show you how to get it right. If there were, the danger would be that you would succeed and show off your longing for God as something to be proud of, maybe something that someone—or better yet, God—would give you a special plaque for.

Don't sit down with your project planner, write your goal at the top of the page—"Develop and recognize a heartfelt longing for God"—and outline the steps you are going to take to achieve it. That's just a way of reigniting the make-something-happen urge that's decidedly unhelpful in a prayerful life with God.

And for heaven's sake, don't get down on yourself for not knowing whether you truly long for God! Remember Premise #1: You do long for God. Remember that even the desire to desire God is a sign of a genuine desire for God because it mirrors God's own desire to be with us. As spiri-tual director Jane Vennard has written, "Sometimes, intimacy with God becomes possible—not because we deserve it or because we have earned it, but because our longing to be with God is a reflection of God's longing to be with us."[3]

Instead of trying to take control, simply begin to *notice*. Watch your life carefully. If grace is waking you up to a longing for God, then keep an eye out for the way that longing presents itself as it walks onto the stage of your life. At first it might just be a simple cameo role, so stay alert; it's likely not yet playing the lead. Note places of dissatisfaction and frustration, of wanting more, of ennui, of restlessness. Places where hope and joy are beginning to bloom. These can all grow from the deep soil of holy desire.

> **TRY THIS:** Pay attention to your longings and desires this week. Write them down. Which ones might be signs of a deepening longing for God?

Or, to change metaphors, imagine that these experiences are large, flat stones, and you can pick them up and look beneath them. Ask yourself what is really beneath this desire or dissatisfaction. What do you see? Will your preferred way of satisfying this longing really work? Or is your spirit perhaps asking for something else in a roundabout way?

Noticing a longing for God might require hitting the pause button on the breathless need to satisfy every urge or escape every unsatisfying inner experience. We must take time to be with these urges and wants before they will take the time to tell us what they are really about. After all, sometimes the urge to eat ice cream at 11:00 p.m. is simply a desire for ice cream; sometimes though, it's a way to escape or distract ourselves from a restlessness that might be an nascent cry for God. It helps to know the difference.

In her memoir *Still: Notes from a Mid-Faith Crisis*, Lauren Winner talks about a period of crisis in her faith following the death of her mother and the breakup of her marriage after five years. She enters a period when she no longer knows how to pray; she doubts the God she has loved and trusted for so long; her old longing for God seems to have disappeared, and she suffers extraordinary loneliness. She says the loneliness makes her want to die, and she'll do anything to avoid it: "call a friend; go shopping; pedal endless, frantic miles on my stationary bike; pour another drink; take another sleeping pill." She tries to escape the dissatisfaction of loneliness.

But Winner has a friend Ruth, a kind and wise soul-friend who speaks into her loneliness: "What Ruth says is: Maybe I should try to stay in the loneliness, just for five minutes, just for ten minutes. Maybe the loneliness has something for me. Maybe I should see what that something is."[4]

Maybe our longings, maybe our experiences of restlessness and our dissatisfactions, maybe our myriad hopes and dreams have something to say to us. Maybe part of that something we long for is intimacy with our divine Source, with the Love that will never let us go. It's just possible these longings we hurry to satisfy or experiences we seek to escape are grace's way of saying, "Look for love; look for the divine love that is at the heart of you— that *is* the heart of you, however hidden it might seem now. *That* is what you really want to find."

Briefly, I'd say two other things.

First, talk to someone about it—a soul friend or spiritual director, a pastor or friend in the faith. Someone who can sit with you and listen, who can discern with you and help you to tease apart the tangled threads of desire balled up in your heart. Someone who can help you to put words to what you are experiencing, give voice to the source of your desire. And someone who won't blush or run from the room when you finally say those words: *I think I want God. More than anything. God.*

And second, finally, give that longing what it wants. Feed it. And what it wants is God. Run, don't walk, to the Source of the grace that's drawing you, and share all you are thinking, feeling, and experiencing. Tell God you are like those deer. Tell God you are hungry and thirsty. As God promises, "Open your mouth wide and I will fill it" (Ps. 81:10).

When you do, you both get what you want: You get God, and God gets you.

A Rich Feast

I pace when I'm preparing to give a talk, not only before I preach. I pace as well before I give a lecture at a retreat, which I do frequently. At retreats sponsored by The Academy for Spiritual Formation, I sometimes find myself giving talks slated for 9:00 a.m., and since breakfast is scheduled for 8:00 a.m. and morning prayer for 7:30 a.m., that means an early start if I'm going to have my hour-long lecture downloaded sufficiently into my brain so that I can roam the lecture platform and engage the audience the way I like.

When I'm at one of these retreats, it's usually with people who have signed up for a two-year program, committing to gather for five days every three months. The main reason people would do that is because of a longing for God, whether that longing shows up dressed as a desire for spiritual experience, growth in community, or a deepening life of prayer. People who seek so much silence, prayer, learning, worship (four times a day), covenant group conversation, and silence (did I mention that?) do so because they believe they will be pointed in the direction of something they've struggled to find elsewhere: a path to the Holy, a way toward the God for whom they long.

After all, the people on these retreats gather for prayer at 7:30 a.m. Every. Single. Day. Before breakfast (but not before coffee). That kind of behavior is not normal.

By the time I wander into prayer, I'm awake. I've had my coffee and paced the floor of my room at the retreat center, quietly rehearsing my talk and timing the forward advance of my lecture slides.

All the retreat centers are different, and I've been to dozens: some rustic, some elegant, some decorated with religious kitsch, some emitting a New Age vibe. But morning prayer always takes place in a worshipful space adorned with icons, candles, and meditatively arranged altar decorations.

We gather in silence, and then we break our silence in unison as we sing praise to God. Quite early in the service of prayer, we do my favorite thing: We sing Psalm 63, a psalm traditionally appointed for morning prayer. This psalm captures perhaps better than any other the human experience of longing for God:

> O God, you are my God, I seek you,
>> my soul thirsts for you;
> my flesh faints for you,
>> as in a dry and weary land where there is no water. (v. 1)

Imagine sixty tired, hungry people, the scent of retreat-center bacon already wafting into the worship space, singing—before they've satisfied any other hunger, except for caffeine—these words that announce the deepest truth of what it means to be human, that speak to the bedrock reality of human existence: Our whole being thirsts for intimacy with God. That thirst drives everything else.

> **TRY THIS:** Meditate on Psalm 63:1-8; then rewrite the psalm in your own words, letting it express your own desire for God.

That's why I love a later line in the psalm: "My soul is satisfied as with a rich feast"—or as the King James Version puts it, "as with marrow and fatness" (v. 5), a more vivid image of the feast. I can't read that line without thinking of medieval feasts, with bannered banquet halls and tables piled with meat, with princes and peasants together eschewing utensils, grabbing turkey legs and digging in.

In this life of frustration, anxiety, and want, we *can* be satisfied. We can taste that for which we long.

Once we know even a hint of what that satisfaction tastes like—the oil of divine solicitude running down our chins—we know the direction to aim our longing. We know that nothing else can compare. *This* is what we've been waiting for. *This* is what we really want.

Such a longing, as one characteristic of a contemplative posture toward praying and living, can strengthen us to stay open, available, and responsive to God.

Right up to the end. Maybe even beyond.

Spiritual Exercises

Sacred Reading

Psalm 42; Psalm 84; Mark 10:46-52
(See directions for sacred reading on page 155.)

Practicing Awareness

Take fifteen minutes and, in a spirit of prayer and with an attitude of openness to God, use these questions to look over yesterday or last week:

- When did I notice a longing for God during this period? How did I know it was a longing for God? How did I respond to the longing?
- When during this period did I resist a longing for God or indulge in desires or longings that were pulling me away from God?
- When did I notice dissatisfaction, frustration, or restlessness? What might these feelings be saying about my life with God?

- What am I learning about my own desire for intimacy with God from what I am noticing in this time of self-examination?

Close with prayer, giving thanks for what God has shown you and asking God to help you be more aware of and responsive to God's loving agency in your life.

Prompts for Journaling

Write a letter to God about your desire for God and how you want that desire to grow. Tell God if there are times when that longing for God seems to disappear or you feel confused about what you really want. Express to God how you would like to respond to your longing for God.

Now, write a letter to yourself *from* God. How do you imagine God would respond to the letter you wrote to God?

3

Savoring Each Sip of Life

Attention

Unless we can pay attention to our experiences for more than a moment, we're likely to miss the ordinary miracles that take place in our lives.

—WILKIE AU, *THE ENDURING HEART*

My wife and I are not wine connoisseurs. We buy it if we like it. And when we discover a wine we like, we stick with it. I drink mostly Prophecy's Pinot Noir, while Ginger prefers Kung Fu Girl's Riesling. We are boring wine drinkers.

But sometimes we branch out.

Fifteen miles from our home, a winery called La Casa Narcisi sits tucked in a hillside. Vine-covered trellises surround the main building, and a Roman style fountain bubbles on a patio. The winery is shooting for a just-outside-of-verdant-Florence look in contrast to its just-outside-of-post-industrial-Pittsburgh reality. Inside at a tasting bar, guests can sample any wine they sell. When we visited, we skimmed the menu, skipped the wines we couldn't pronounce, and settled on two we wanted to taste: peach and black raspberry.

The sommelier poured peach wine into two glasses.

"I like this," I said. I glanced at Ginger.

"So do I," she said.

Then we tried the black raspberry.

"I like this," Ginger said, eyebrows raised.

I nodded in agreement. "So do I."

We bought a bottle of each. As I told you, we're not sophisticated wine drinkers.

But some people are. They've trained their palates to detect any hint of flavor in a wine. To become a sommelier takes years of study and training. A good sommelier—after considering its look (cloudy? clear?), smell (earthy? woody?), and taste (sweet? acidic? fruity?)—should be able to determine the provenance of any wine and the variety of its grapes.

You've seen the process. The taster swirls the wine in a glass, watching how it clings to the inside of the glass as it slides back down. Then they stick their nose in the glass, inhaling with eyes closed. Then they taste, taking five minutes to swallow so that the wine coats every taste bud, and so that, you suspect, they have time to make up the ridiculous things they are about to say. Finally, they offer their conclusion: "I taste hints of oak, blueberry, hibiscus, and wild mushroom in this wine from the northernmost region of the province of Anjou, France."

And you're thinking, *They're making this up.* You expect them to go on and predict your future: *You'll have a job change soon and enter a satisfying relationship.* All from a sip of wine.

But they're not joking.

The difference between me and a sommelier—besides their apron and bow tie—is the quality of attention. They approach each sip with an informed attention honed by experience, open to whatever notes of flavor it offers. For a sommelier, whether they *like* the wine is irrelevant.

A posture of openness, availability, and responsiveness to God in life and prayer helps us to become the sommeliers of our own lives: to learn to see, smell, feel each note of Divine Presence, to taste the full flavor of grace infusing each moment of our lives. We are invited to sip the wine of our lives with attention and care. Imagine approaching the rich texture of life with that kind of attention. Imagine the often bland and foggy moments of life becoming focused and sharp because of the attention we bring to them.

Imagine changing a child's diaper that way, or kissing a lover. Washing the dishes or raking the leaves. Doing your taxes or sitting in prayer. Imagine how you might appreciate these experiences afresh when they are approached with expectant attention. Imagine how you might discover God's grace in them.

> **CONSIDER THIS:** How would you describe your current level of attention to your life? to God? to others?

"Listen to your life," Frederick Buechner writes. "See it for the fathomless mystery that it is. In the boredom and pain of it no less than in the excitement and gladness: touch, taste, smell your way to the holy and hidden heart of it because in the last analysis all moments are key moments, and life itself is grace."[1]

So maybe we should pay attention. Apron and bow tie optional.

What Gets in the Way?

While we might be able to *imagine* paying that kind of attention to our lives and God's presence in them, most of us will admit that we don't approach life that way.

Before we explore the possibilities of attention, it's worth asking why we don't. What gets in the way?

The first answer is *the nature of our minds*. Our minds think, plan, perseverate. They ruminate on the past, worry about the future. It's what they do. We evolved to be hyper-vigilant to danger. We live on high alert, always scanning our environment, imagining the spectral figures of disease, financial ruin, job loss—the list goes on—lurking around the next corner. When early humans were living in caves, daily facing the potential of death by bear or tiger, this feature of our brains kept us alive. Now the likelihood of an alpha predator stalking our every move has significantly decreased, but our minds haven't adapted to our new reality. We continue to scan, fear, worry. Much of what stalks us now is the long-over past or an unknown future. Perhaps this is the reason Jesus admonished us to live like lilies—enjoying the present and abandoning the self in trust to God—rather than practicing that peculiarly human trait unknown to the rest of the animal kingdom: worrying about what tomorrow will bring (see Matthew 6:25-34).

We also have a *desire to distract ourselves from our pain*. In his book *Food: A Love Story*, Jim Gaffigan writes about his love of eating. He says that he's never been hungry because he's always eating, usually cheese. Then he notes wryly, "It's either that or feel my feelings."[2] For many of us, feeling our feelings—attending to the fear, guilt, grief, and anxiety always bubbling just beneath the surface of our lives, ever threatening to burst forth like a geyser—seems like a horrible idea.

Why would I want to do that? we think. *Pass the Havarti.*

But if life is grace, as Buechner says, then we miss a great deal when there are whole dimensions of our lives we are unwilling or unable to acknowledge. We miss the possibility that God might be in those feelings to teach and strengthen, encourage and heal. Grace might be bubbling alongside them beneath the surface; it might burst forth as well.

Years ago, I enrolled in an eight-week mindfulness-based stress reduction course at a university medical center. Everything I'd read suggested that a practice of mindfulness could lesson my symptoms of anxiety. On the first night, fifteen of us sat in a room that had rocks stacked Jedi-like and pillows piled in the corners. The instructor said the only thing during the course I remember verbatim: "It's going to get worse before it gets better." *Does she want us to come back?* I wondered. Yes, but she also wanted us to understand that we're likely to feel worse for a time when we finally lay aside the habits of distracting ourselves from our pain and anxiety and begin to pay attention. Not because the anxiety and pain are *actually* worse, but because we've let ourselves become of aware of them, maybe for the first time.

It gets worse before it gets better. No wonder we don't want to pay attention to our pain.

Finally, at the risk of seeming an old codger (which my children think I already am, with my gray sneakers, baggy khakis, and cardigan sweater), I must mention that *digital technology and social media exploit the nature of our minds* and our desire to distract ourselves to keep us laser-focused on our devices, like indoor cats mesmerized by squirrels in the yard. The neuroscientific research is conclusive: Our technology is designed to stimulate the reward center of the brain, so that we simply can't stop checking our devices to make sure we're not missing something—a breaking headline, a notification that someone "likes" one of our photos, or a new video of cute cats watching squirrels in the yard. Social media platforms like Facebook and streaming services like Netflix are what Jake Knapp and John Zeratsky, authors of *Making Time*, call "Infinity Pools" because they always have new content; the mesmerized user never has a reason to look away. Their potential to distract is inexhaustible.[3]

> **CONSIDER THIS:**
> Which of the three obstacles to attention (see pp. 54–55) is most prevalent in your life? What other obstacles are you aware of?

If we want to see our lives for the fathomless mysteries they are, we will have to address our relationship to technology and social media. We don't necessarily need to eliminate them. Just last night, I spent fifteen minutes engaged in a Facebook exchange with three old college friends. Alone at my desk, I laughed as I recalled our shared antics. For that moment, I was able to give thanks for social media.

But I don't need to respond instantly to every new post, comment, or like. I can turn off notifications. I can remove distracting apps from my phone or from the home screen. I can stash my phone in another room. I can enjoy the sabbath social-media free. I can cultivate other ways of connecting with distant friends: writing letters, placing phone calls, scheduling road trips.

> **TRY THIS:** Put your phone or tablet in a drawer for a few hours, and pay attention to how this feels. How often do you wish you had it? What difference does this distance from your device(s) make?

I can be increasingly attentive to the way I'm using technology so that it's not using me. Freed from its grasp, I can then begin to address the other two obstacles to attentiveness: the way my busy mind keeps me focused on everything but the present, and the way the pain and anxiety of the present make me want to check my phone or run to the fridge for cheese.

Attention in Daily Life

Simone Weil, a twentieth-century philosopher and mystic, wrote one of the most quoted lines in the history of spirituality: "[A]ttention . . . is the very substance of prayer."[4] Every recent book on spirituality I can think of quotes this line, including my own.

When I was writing a book on midlife spirituality, a writing workshop leader read a draft, saw that I used the Weil quotation above, and told me to take it out. "That old chestnut," she said, "has become a cliché." A couple of years later I read a review this workshop leader wrote of a new collection of essays. She spotted this line of Weil's in the book and chided the author: "There's a subgenre in which quotations like these are so frequently quoted that they seem clichés. . . . I want [the author] to show me something in them that I don't already know how to see."[5] The author criticized in the review is a well-regarded essayist, so I felt like I was in good company.

Maybe the reason many people don't investigate more deeply the substance of Weil's adage is that it's buried in an essay titled "Reflections on the Right Use of School Studies with a View to the Love of God"—hardly a click-bait title. In that essay, Weil suggests that the "quality of attention counts for much in the quality of the prayer,"[6] and she wants to show us that attention can be trained. We have the capacity to grow our attention, and it doesn't require meditative calisthenics. She uses schoolwork as a case study to show we can hone our attention in daily life. Weil says that students should learn to like all the subjects they study because "all of them develop that faculty of attention which, directed toward God, is the very substance of prayer."[7]

As a professor, I know many students will reject Weil's statement. My own fifteen-year-old son, just a week ago, marched out of his bedroom and announced, "I hate it when teachers say, 'It's not the grade that matters;

it's what you learn.' Of course it's the grade that matters!" Weil writes as if responding directly to him:

> Students must therefore work without any wish to gain good marks, to pass examinations, to win school successes; without any reference to their natural abilities and tastes; applying themselves equally to all their tasks, with the idea that each one will help to form in them the habit of that attention which is the substance of prayer.[8]

While Weil might not find a sympathetic reading among teenagers, her fundamental insight rings true and can speak to those of us who are, thankfully, no longer students: All of life can provide a training ground for attention.

CONSIDER THIS: How do you react to the point Simone Weil is making about attention and prayer? Is this a new idea to you?

Right now, for instance, I'm sitting on my back patio. It's a summer morning, and my back yard is providing a feast for my attention: the copious honeysuckle twining along the fence, its yellow and white trumpet-shaped blossoms waiting for my daughter to come taste their nectar; the squirrel we call Sam chittering in the sassafras tree, noisily announcing his presence; a steady wind rustling the leaves; the chair next to me rocking in the wind as if a ghost has joined me for a chat. I notice the wind tickling my cheek, reminding me that I'm here now, that I'm alive, reminding me as Jesus said that God's Spirit blows where she will like the wind, out of our control (see John 3:8). All we can do is pay attention.

I always have the option of checking out, of course. I can check my email on my phone. I can get lost in the cocktail party in my mind or peruse my mental curio cabinet of worries. I can start thinking about when

I'll grade papers, how I'll write about this experience later today, or how I'll lead next week's online intensive class. There's a time for that kind of planning, to be sure, and when that time comes, I hope I will give the work my fullest attention. But now is not that time. Right now the call is to return to the present, where the gift of summer is unfolding before me, where God's Spirit is gently blowing, where my own life is being lived.

All of life is a school of attention. And school is always in session.

Attention and Our Neighbors

Simone Weil says there's a further reason we should live with a posture of attention: Not only does a prayerful love of God consist of attention; love of our neighbors does as well. We avoid the pain of others as eagerly as we distract ourselves from our own. Yet, Weil writes, "Those who are unhappy have no need of anything in this world but people capable of giving them their attention. The capacity to give one's attention to a sufferer is a very rare and difficult thing; it is almost a miracle; it *is* a miracle."[9] Compassion requires a posture of attention.

Before Weil said this, Jesus showed it.

Jesus, his disciples, and a crowd were approaching Jericho (see Mark 10:46-52). Maybe they had some place to be; they seemed to be on a tight schedule. The disciples, who saw themselves as Jesus' handlers, were no doubt hurrying Jesus to his next gig. But a man who was blind and was begging on the roadside heard the crowds, learned Jesus was approaching, and began to shout, "Jesus, Son of David, have mercy on me!" (v. 47). Jesus' handlers shushed the man. This was no time for Jesus to get sidetracked. So he shouted louder, and Jesus heard him.

Jesus "stood still," the scripture says (v. 49). I imagine a dramatic pause as the crowd wondered what would happen next. Perhaps Jesus was absorbing the sound of the man's cry, paying full attention to the pain in his voice. Then Jesus invited the man forward. When the man got to Jesus, Jesus asked him, "What do you want me to do for you?" (v. 51). And I can imagine everything else fell away as Jesus looked in this man's face. That question was like telling the man, "You have my full attention. You might as well be the only person in the world right now. You are my present reality." In story after story, Jesus sees and attends to those in pain, those whom society has cast to the margins because their suffering was unbearable to watch.

> **TRY THIS:** Make a list of the people in your life to whom you could more fully give your attention. Pray for these people, and ask God to help you to be more attentive to them in your interactions.

Sometimes I imagine God as that beggar, sitting on the side of the road and calling to us through our own fears, hopes, and struggles; calling to us through the fears, hopes, and struggles of others. The question to ask ourselves if we want to be open, available, and responsive to God is this: Will we stand still long enough to pay attention?

Paying Attention in Prayer

I sat with students in a circle in room 216. A small table was centered in the middle of our circle, draped with a green scarf. A faux candle flickered on the table because the seminary's insurance policy wouldn't let me light a real one. We'd come to my favorite part of the introduction to spiritual formation course—student-led spiritual practices. After eight months of my leading prayer each week, it was finally the students' turn. They were the ones inviting us to close our eyes and take deep cleansing breaths. They were the ones instructing us to whisper a prayer in the silence of our hearts for the person sitting next to us. They were the ones encouraging us to draw our prayers with crayons, trace our way through a finger-labyrinth, or listen to scripture with ears open to the Spirit.

The scripture that morning was the story from Luke's Gospel of Jesus' sending out seventy disciples two-by-two to witness through word and deed to God's kingdom (see Luke 10:1-20). He told them to take nothing with them and depend on the hospitality of others, even if that meant eating food that was unclean. "Eat what is set before you," he told them (v. 8).

That morning in class Jesus told me the same thing. When my student read that line, I felt tears sting my eyes. I knew I had to pause and pay attention. Had I been feeling dissatisfied with life? Bored in my job? Frustrated with one thing after another? If so, I hadn't known it until that moment, hadn't paid attention to how my restlessness and anxiety had been inching up in the previous months. But it was as if Jesus were sitting there next to me, whispering in my ear, "Eat what is set before you. Take the life that you've got and be nourished by it. Sip the wine of your life and enjoy. Don't feel like you have to hurry off to something new. There's joy in the table already set for you. I promise."

The students had done such a good job creating the space for my attentiveness in prayer, I was open to hearing the Spirit speak to me through scripture. I noticed how that line struck me, how it moved me to tears. I paid attention and listened to God's Spirit speaking through

> **CONSIDER THIS:** Do you have times set aside for prayer and attention to God? If not, what would it take to begin?

my innermost self. As I left class that day, I walked back into this life I've been given with a different perspective, looking for the nourishment—the grace—in it all.

When we make time for prayer, we say to God what Jesus in essence said to the man who was blind and begging on the side of the road: *You have my complete attention.* And when we give God our attention, we shouldn't be surprised to hear God speak.

Almost every spiritual practice is a practice of attention. In prayer we set aside a few minutes each day to attend openly to God. While everyday contemplatives long to be attentive to God throughout life, that attention is our primary activity when we pray. In times of prayer, we want to be present to God's presence, to attune ourselves to God's voice.

That means we can't be in a hurry. Like a sommelier savoring a sip of wine, we savor words, phrases, and images when we are praying with scripture. When we receive Holy Communion, we walk slowly up the sanctuary aisle, feeling the press of every step into the floor, noticing the texture of the bread in our cupped hand, the wet of wine or juice on our lips, the scratch of an "Amen" in our own throats. When we are praying in silence, we bring our attention to our breath, which stabilizes the mind and helps us to let go of all the intruding thoughts that want to steal our attention from God's presence. In all these ways, we say to God, *I'm here, and you are all I want right now.*

We can practice this kind of prayerful attention retrospectively as well. That is what the practice called the Daily Examen facilitates. Ignatius of Loyola, the sixteenth-century founder of the Jesuits, taught that nothing was more important than pausing each day to look for signs of God's love and our own response to that love. During an Examen, we look back through a particular period and ask ourselves questions like the following: *When did I notice God's Spirit in my life? For what in this period of time do I have to be thankful? How have I resisted God's ways, resisted the call to love? For what do I need God's guidance?* The questions vary, but the point remains the same—to notice and savor the presence of God's grace and become increasingly aware of how we respond to that grace in the moment. An Examen can be performed at the end of the day, week, or month. Whenever we do it, the Examen focuses our attention on the movement of God in our lives. The more we practice attending to God retrospectively, the better we become at attending to God in the moment.

Whatever the practice—meditating on scripture, walking a labyrinth, coloring a mandala, contemplating with prayer beads, praying the psalms, or any of a hundred other ways of prayer—one movement of attention runs through them all: return. Any time we are praying, we will

> **TRY THIS:** Do a brief Examen over the previous twenty-four hours. What do you notice? What sticks out to you?

find ourselves getting sucked into the cocktail party in our minds. We will get lost in thoughts about the past, worry about the future, or any of the many inane fantasies our minds can conjure without provocation. As soon as we realize we have stopped paying attention to our praying and have chased a tempting thought, we simply return to the task at hand. We gently and without judgment lead our attention back to the practice of prayer—back to the words on the page, our feet tracing the labyrinth's path, the marker brightening the surface of the page, the beads in our hand, or the prayer word we're repeating as we walk.

There's more to each of these practices than attention—the things that make each way of prayer unique—but attention is the substance of prayer and is at the heart of them all.

An Attentive God

At the beginning of this chapter, I suggested we might want to become the sommeliers of our own lives, deeply attentive to even the subtlest details because in them we might discern hints of the Divine. We can be encouraged in paying that kind of attention by receiving some good news: God shows that kind of attention to us; God knows our lives intimately and delights in us.

This is a truth the book of Psalms affirms more than once.

One psalm declares that the One who watches over Israel "will neither slumber nor sleep" (121:4). Our own attention can wane when we become tired, but God's eyelids never get heavy; God never rests from considering us in love.

Another favorite psalm says we can't escape the searching gaze of God's love. Whether we fly into the heavens or hide in the deeps or take cover in the shadows, the light of God's love is present with us (see Psalm 139:7-12). When we want to hide, afraid of our own rebellion and guilt, we can rest assured that God's attentive gaze is filled with love and take comfort in the truth that God is the author of kindness, compassion, and mercy.

Jesus said not one of the millions of sparrows falls from the sky without God's compassionate knowledge (see Matthew 10:29). How much more valuable are you and I to God? So attentive is God that God knows the number of hairs on each of our heads. If God is this attentive to my life, maybe that means my life is worth my attention. If God pays compassionate attention to my neighbors, maybe they are worthy of my compassionate attention as well. Rooted in the love of an attentive God, our own attentive love of ourselves and others can begin to flourish.

In the spring, my ten-year-old daughter and I were climbing the hill to our house at the end of a long walk. All of creation seemed to be blooming—buds on the dogwood trees, daffodils in the yards, forsythia ablaze in gold. I was stopped by the aroma of what I think were lilacs, though I never located the origin of the scent on that breezy day. We just stood there in the middle of the road, no doubt looking silly to the neighbors as we stood with our faces pointed up, sniffing and sniffing the air.

"That's so wonderful. I don't remember smelling this before," I said.

"Well, Dad, you must not have been paying attention because it smells this way every year."

I'm sure she was right. These fragrances didn't materialize for the first time that week. But work, stress, worry—that out-of-control habit of thinking—had kept me asleep to this gift, unaware.

Until now.

So we walked up the hill slowly, taking it in. I was making up for lost springs, determined never to miss this again.

As I remember this, I'm thankful that, though our attention wanes and we fall asleep, the Holy One walking beside us each moment of our lives never loses track of us. "The LORD has been mindful of us; he will bless us" (Ps. 115:12).

God is mindful of us—that *is* the blessing.

Spiritual Exercises

Sacred Reading

Psalm 139; Psalm 121; Luke 13:10-17
(See directions for sacred reading on page 155.)

Practicing Awareness

Take an "attention walk." Walk through your neighborhood, a nearby downtown area, or a park or nature reserve. (If getting outside is difficult, this exercise can be done at home or sitting in a room.) As you begin, ask the Holy Spirit to help you walk with a heart that is open and available to God in all that you see, feel, and hear. Walk slowly, and simply pay attention. Try to walk for thirty minutes to an hour. Let all your senses be engaged.

- What do you see as you walk? Allow your eyes to scan slowly the environment. Pause on occasion to look around.
- What do you smell, feel, or hear? Pause and savor these experiences.
- What is going on inside of you as you walk? What feelings or emotions do you notice? Gladness? Anxiety? Do you feel relaxed or nervous? Just pay attention without judging these feelings.
- What is going on in your mind? When you find yourself lost in thought, simply bring your attention back to the world around you.

When you are finished, reflect on what you experienced. How was this different from your usual way of being in life? Can you approach more of your life with this kind of attention? Did you have a sense that God was speaking to you through anything you experienced? Spend some time in prayer, sharing with God what you noticed, asking for insight, and resting in God's presence.

Prompts for Journaling

Write a letter to God about your desire to be more attentive to your own life, to others, and to God's presence in both. Be honest with God about what stands in the way of your being more present in your life. Share with God about your practices of prayer and how you would like to be more aware of God's presence through them. Ask for God's help. Share whatever is on your heart regarding your attention to God in your daily life.

Now, write a letter to yourself *from* God. How do you imagine God would respond to the letter you wrote to God?

4

Trading Willfulness for Willingness

Patience

Above all, trust in the slow work of God. . . . Give Our
Lord the benefit of believing that his hand is leading you,
and accept the anxiety of feeling yourself in suspense and
incomplete.

—Pierre Teilhard de Chardin, SJ

For more than a decade, I've been a part of the organization I mentioned in the previous chapter, The Academy for Spiritual Formation. The Academy offers a program with five-day retreats every three months for two years. I first experienced this program as a participant and then as a faculty presenter.

On the second-to-last night of each retreat, the leadership team hosts a service of prayer and healing. I've now attended more than thirty of these services, and until a few years ago, I'd often request prayers for the same outcome: healing. When I was a senior in college, I was diagnosed with a form of arthritis called *ankylosing spondylitis*, a disease that attacks the hips, spine, neck, and ribs. The pain can be sharp and intense. I limped every day for a year before my diagnosis.

I was speaking at one of these retreats a few years ago, and my arthritis flared up. I hadn't brought my cane—I bought my first cane in my early twenties—and I was struggling to stand and walk, not good for a peripatetic lecturer like myself. Compassionate retreatants poured sympathy on me. One found a gnarled branch in the woods for me to use as a walking stick. One of the leaders kidnapped me, drove me to her cabin, and forced me to ingest a natural supplement she swore would help—two rough, white pills I'm almost sure were legal. She's not a woman you say no to.

By the healing service the next night, the medicinal supplements hadn't worked, which made them no different from all the healing prayers over the years. But still I limped to the service, staff in hand. While the community sang the songs of Taizé in a room flickering with candles, icons of saints glowing in the wavery light, I hobbled to a prayer station in a corner and sat down. Two of my friends sat across from me. One anointed my head with oil in the name of the Father, Son, and Holy Spirit, and the other laid a hand on my shoulder and asked how he could pray for me.

It was time to do again what I'd done so many times before, even though precedent suggested I would be limping out as I had limped in.

But what came out of my mouth surprised me. "I need prayers for patience," I said. "I want to discover how to live with this arthritis as part of my life, rather than always fighting it. I'd like you to pray that I might be more open to seeing God's presence in this with me and that being patient with pain might make room for the Spirit to transform me in love." Or something along those lines, maybe less articulate, less lofty at the end, less pious—I was muttering the request through sniffles and tears, after all.

Sitting in that chair, perhaps inspired by the God in whose name I'd just been anointed, I had a realization: If I was going to live a life open and responsive to God, I would need to learn to face reality as it is rather than as I want it to be. That would mean approaching my life with patience—the patience required to live not in control. The patience required to notice and even welcome the guests in my life—some invited, some not—that play a role in the drama of my days.

I needed the patience to see what a response of love might look like as it emerges from a spirit tutored by chronic pain.

I would need to adopt a posture of patience.

The Heart of Impatience

When I was a child, the children and youth of our church performed a musical in which I was cast as a father snail doling out unwanted advice to my snail child. I sang my paternal wisdom nervously since I could never get right one interval in the melody (I still can't today as I sing it here at my desk). In the song I urged the younger snail to have patience, telling him not to hurry so much but to remember that even God is patient.

The song captures what many take to be the heart of patience: going slow, not being in a hurry. This need to slow down has become a clichéd mantra in our culture. Thus the manifold *slow* movements: slow food, slow living, even a slow fashion movement, whatever that could possibly be. I have a book on my shelf titled *The Slow Professor*. And going slow *is* a part of patience. We can only attend well to our lives, as I suggested in the previous chapter, when we slow to a pace that allows us to notice the particulars of our lives, and we can only attend to God in our spiritual practices if we refuse the temptation to hurry.

But approaching patience this way can also lead to moralism. Patience becomes an imperative—something you owe to others, a wagging finger telling you to slow down. This is the shadow side of patience.

If we peer more deeply into situations in which we find ourselves getting impatient, noticing the way that impatience can transform into frustration that can boil over into anger, we'll discover the real difficulty doesn't lie in going too slow but in being out of control. We get impatient when the reigns of control are wrested from our grip—or when we learn we never held them. When we're stymied, we don't become impatient because we're not going as *fast* as we want but because we are not going as fast as *we want*—a subtle but significant distinction.

The Pittsburgh International Airport is twenty-nine miles from my home, and no route leads there other than through downtown Pittsburgh. At the wrong time of day, that trip takes more than an hour. I always leave three hours before my flight. Last January, I had to fly to Virginia to lead a retreat. I left plenty early, and not five miles from my house the traffic came to a standstill. My traffic app could not find a route that would take less than two hours. I didn't know what to be more worried about, missing my flight or not being near a restroom as my morning coffee filtered through my system. When I finally arrived at the airport, I parked in the hourly parking (my apologies to the organization that reimbursed my travel—no time to catch a shuttle from the cheaper extended lot), dashed into the airport with my roller bag bouncing wildly behind me, hurried in and out of a restroom, and took my place in the security line just as my flight was beginning to board.

> **TRY THIS:** Write a paragraph about a time when you felt out of control. What was it like? How did you approach the situation? How would you like your approach to be different now?

While I sat stuck in my car, not going anywhere and compulsively checking the time, I grew impatient. As I stood delayed in the security line, nervously glancing at the departures screen, my impatience increased. Did I become impatient because I was going slow or because I was going slow and didn't want to? I was chafing at a lack of control.

The little snail is in a hurry, but by nature he's slow; the father sees his frustration and says, "Be patient." He's saying a lot with those words, but most profoundly he's inviting his child to live at peace with a world he can't control, a lesson that will serve him well his whole life. If he chooses to listen.

> **CONSIDER THIS:** What do you think about the distinction between patience as "going slow" and patience as "learning to be out of control"? Does that distinction have any meaning in how you think about times when you become impatient?

The Heart of Patience

For years I've borrowed the concept of "willed passivity" from the beloved pastor and author Eugene Peterson to name the quality of patience marked by equanimity with being out of control.[1] But that term takes a lot of explaining. *Willed passivity*? For one thing, we hate the very notion of passivity, of not being the primary agents in our lives. But Peterson says living well with God requires acknowledging that most of life happens to us—a reality of being human in a world we didn't create and where others exercise agency as well. Peterson invites us to imagine what it would be like to honor that truth, especially in our life before God—thus the adjective *willed*. We can choose to adopt a posture toward life and God that recognizes our essential out-of-control-ness. We can either approach reality defiantly, like modern Don Quixotes fighting windmills, or we can receive life as it comes to us and embrace it, honoring the gifts and limits of our own agency and neither over- nor underestimating our capacity to control events.

We can receive reality with an openness of spirit, equanimity, and an eye open for God's presence because we're not constantly distracted by our anger over the fact that things aren't the way we want them.

Peterson points to Jesus as an exemplar of willed passivity. As Jesus approached the hour of his crucifixion, he "steadfastly set his face to go to Jerusalem," willingly accepting the future as it unfolded before him (Luke 9:51, kjv). Though he wept in the garden of Gethsemane, he affirmed, "Not my will, but thine, be done" (Luke 22:42, kjv). Notice he didn't passively roll over; he used his own agency to accept a will other than his own. He also said, "No one takes [my life] from me, but I lay it down of my own accord" (John 10:18). Because the last days of Jesus' life paint a picture of being out of control and because he was largely silent before Pilate (see Matthew 27:14), Christians have long associated a verse from Isaiah with Jesus: "Like a lamb that is led to the slaughter, and like a sheep that before its shearers is silent, so he did not open his mouth" (53:7). Stripped, beaten, nailed to a cross, he actively accepted the cost of living such an open, loving, fully human life: rejection and death. His crucifixion shows the depths of his engagement with life, evil, and sin. In allowing himself to die, he was participating in God's creative and surprising response to the world's rebellious desire for control.

But after years of struggling to explain to puzzled audiences the paradox of willed passivity, I began searching for another way to put it. I was talking on the phone not long ago with a friend who, at almost twice my age, has grappled with these issues longer than I. I told him what I liked about Peterson's phrase but that it wasn't ideal for getting at the essential quality of patience. He said that he'd always appreciated psychiatrist and spiritual director Gerald May's notion of "willingness." "There's a chapter on willingness in his book *Will and Spirit*. You might want to look at it," he said. I took his advice and read the book.

May contrasts what he calls *willingness* with *willfulness*. Willfulness, he says, "is the setting of oneself apart from the fundamental essence of life in an attempt to master, direct, control, or otherwise manipulate existence."[2] Someone who is willful—that is, most of us most of the time—approaches life with agendas, and an agenda is just another way of saying "the way *I* want it." When our willfulness is frustrated—when we don't get what we want—our ability to master, direct, control, or manipulate the course of life is revealed as a sham. And we become impatient.

In my experience, this often happens in airports and when dealing with young children.

Willingness is subtler. Willingness names a positive engagement, not a dull, get-walked-all-over-like-a-doormat approach to life, while it surrenders the illusion of control. It recognizes that our lives are involved in what May calls "some ultimate cosmic process"[3] that the Divine Presence works in all that is, and we can live as participants in that process, working with the grain of peace, justice, and love as a woodworker works with the grain of the wood. Willingness says yes to life as it comes, while willfulness says "yes, but . . ." May explains:

> It is obvious we cannot say yes to everything we encounter; many specific things and situations in life are terribly destructive and must be resisted. But willingness and willfulness do not apply to specific things or situations. They reflect instead the underlying attitude one has toward the wonder of life itself. Willingness notices this wonder and bows in some kind of reverence of it.[4]

Willingness surrenders the narrow, willful agendas of our egos and enters the flow of divine goodness, allowing our chosen participation in that divine life to enable our faithful agency in the world.

CONSIDER THIS: When in your life are you most likely to live willfully? When are you most able to live willingly? How do these life postures feel different to you?

Patience, I believe, does the same. It pauses, notices the habits of self-assertion that drive so many of our responses to life—often when frustration arises because our self-assertion has been thwarted—and releases the need to master, control, and manipulate.

Patience asks, "What might an engagement with reality—with this moment—look like if I'm open to grace, love, and beauty right now and as they unfold?"

Even in airports. Even when dealing with young children.

When God Goes Too Slow

So we can imagine a posture of patient willingness when we face frustrating circumstances. But what about when *God* moves too slowly? When *God* fails to cooperate with our heartfelt desires?

If we exert little control in most of our lives, we exert none over God.

The Christian faith proclaims transformation. A popular bumper sticker says, "Christians aren't better, just forgiven." That tells only half the story. The other half sings of how God's grace brings restoration—makes us *better*. In the chapter on longing, I said we long for God because God created us in God's own image, and like seeks like. But Christians also believe the divine image in us has become distorted, often by our own willful refusal to be what God has made us to be—a refusal otherwise known as sin. The image needs to be renewed. That original divine image is being healed in us when grace renews us in the image of Christ. The word *salvation* comes from a word that means to heal. Salvation involves more than forgiveness, more than having the slate wiped clean. It involves restoration and transformation.

God owns the work of transformation. God renews. God restores. God heals. Just as God created the world through Christ, so God accomplishes our re-creation through Christ. We of course have a role to play in that re-creation, a grace-enabled role to participate with God and consent to what God is doing. God takes the lead; we respond to the work of the Spirit. As we respond and increasingly yield to God's saving care, we begin to embody the image of Christ; we grow in our love of God and in sacrificial service to our neighbor.

> **CONSIDER THIS:**
> How have you typically thought about salvation? Has it included the idea of transformation and healing?

But God does not always work according to our schedule.

This isn't a problem when things are going well—when worship brings consolation and spiritual fruit springs readily from the soil of our soul, or when delight in God and ease in prayer refresh our spirits. How easily patience comes when God is cooperating with us! How comfortable consent is when we see the fruit and feel the joy! Then words of surrender come effortlessly to our lips. We gladly give the divine Potter free rein.

But sometimes for reasons we don't understand, the journey slows, and pleasant experiences of prayer and joy in life with God disappear. Clouds block the warm sun of grace. Brambles block the way forward. We enter a wilderness, and God seems absent. We wonder, *Where has the promise of a peace that passes understanding gone? Why has the journey of transformation seemed to stop?*

When patience gets tested this way, that's when the posture matters the very most. So we wait. We hope. We approach prayer with an open, willing spirit. We trust that this period marks a work of grace so deep in our spirits that we can't see it—because if we could we would likely resist. Maybe in a hidden way, God is freeing us from our need to control, liberating us from our deep-seated willfulness.

I find myself getting impatient with God when I perceive that the journey isn't moving fast enough and the transformation isn't total enough. Thomas Merton famously wrote, "For me to be a saint means to be myself."[5] Sometimes I cry to God: *Why am I not yet my truest self? Why am I not yet a saint? Let's get on with it!* Expressing our desire to God for change—for renewal in our own lives and in the broken world around us—is an appropriate aspect of patience, modeled on the plea of Jesus in the garden of Gethsemane and the cries of despair in the Psalms when God appeared to be taking God's sweet time to right the wrongs of injustice.

> **TRY THIS:** Write a prayer to God expressing your own desire for transformation. Be as honest as you can.

Teresa of Avila's *Interior Castle* describes the seven mansions through which the soul journeys toward union with God. I've read the book many times over the years even though I always get frustrated that mansions one and two, the ones furthest from the center, describe my usual stomping grounds. *When will I get to mansion three? Let alone to mansion seven where union with God happens.* Teresa herself didn't imagine the journey through these mansions to be swift or linear, but that is of little comfort when I feel this way.

So, our pleas have an appropriate place in our patient posture toward God.

For my own begging plea, I adopt a verse from Charles Wesley's hymn "Love Divine, All Loves Excelling":

Finish, then, thy new creation; pure and spotless let us be.

Let us see thy great salvation perfectly restored in thee;

changed from glory into glory, till in heaven we take our place,
till we cast our crowns before thee, lost in wonder, love, and praise.[6]

That verse voices my longing like no other. Who would look around—into the recesses of our own souls and out toward a world that's marred by injustice and menaced by violence—and not cry out to God? Patience doesn't preclude our cries; it includes them. Patience that cries to God is simply being honest.

While I'll never stop praying that hymn verse—never stop pleading for God to get on with it—I know in my depths that I most deeply want to consent to what God is doing even when I can't see it and don't understand it. When the impatient urge to wrest control from God for the forward march of spiritual transformation strikes, I need the Holy Spirit to remind me of a prayer by Howard Thurman, a mystic and one of the fathers of the civil rights movement, in which he prays to live in God's sense of time. He admits his general anxiety, his hurry to accomplish projects, and his living with a lack of patience. He confesses that he can't tell when to wait and when to hurry "because my sense of time is dulled." He asks God to give him the perspective to live with a "profound sense of leisure" and to help him move through his days with a sense of God's time.[7]

Our patience can grow when we allow our pleas for justice and longing for transformation to walk hand-in-hand with prayers like Thurman's—prayers of consent, prayers for a divine perspective on our hurry, prayers for freedom from the need to control.

Receiving the Gift of Patience

You're sitting in a meeting. The room has no windows. The plastic chair aggravates your sciatica. You can't think of a good excuse to leave, but as your coworker drones on, the ineffectual chairperson fails to steer the meeting back on course. The bowl of peanuts is empty, as is your coffee cup. You have a long to-do list, and you can't check anything off as you sit here unable to escape. You start getting fidgety, even angry. Your frustration builds. What do you do?

Well, here's what I sometimes do: get frustrated at my frustration, angry with my anger, impatient with my impatience. Much of the time.

But sometimes—by grace—I have the presence of mind simply to notice what's going on inside me: *I see you—urge to run out of the room; I feel you—anger rising in my throat; I acknowledge you—frustrated desire to take charge.* Then I might whisper a prayer: "God, here I am, and here you are. Help me be open to the possibility in this room. Help me see how I can respond to this moment authentically and faithfully. Help me to learn what this situation has to teach." I re-engage the meeting. I ask a question. I make a suggestion. I calmly note we're off track.

> **TRY THIS:** Have a conversation with someone about situations (like meetings) in which you are prone to impatience. Brainstorm creative and constructive responses to those situations that avoid vainly grasping for control.

One possible response to feeling trapped and out of control—feeling as if the precious moments of your life are being stolen, crumpled, and tossed into the rubbish—is to slip into willfulness: reject what's going on and strategize control. This will often fail, and failure inflames impatience.

The other possibility is to relax and receive the gift of patience. You can't force patience—*forced patience* is a true oxymoron. But it can be received, learned over time, and practiced. And it starts by noticing, by paying attention to the impatience creeping around in your spirit. As soon as you notice it, it has less control over you. Nod to it. Smile at it. Call it an old friend. Take a slow breath and welcome it. That way you disarm the impatience.

Then remind yourself that God is here, and even this moment, whatever the moment entails, is full of possibility and potential because of God's presence. It may not be the potential for what *you* want to happen (for a meeting to end immediately, for example, so you can get your own agenda for the day back on track), but it is potential nonetheless: potential for grace, compassion, and wisdom to flower; potential for you to exercise your freedom and agency in appropriate ways; potential for something right and good to happen. Receiving the gift of patience opens you to the possibility of this potential, a possibility guaranteed by the presence of an infinitely creative God.

There's a reason the apostle Paul calls patience a fruit of the Spirit (see Galatians 5:22).

> **CONSIDER THIS:** What do you think it means to call patience a fruit of the Spirit? How have you sensed that fruit growing in you?

Living Out of Control

A year and a half ago, shortly after I turned forty-three, I concluded that I should take charge of my health. Too many days I didn't feel like shooting baskets or playing tennis with my son, and my energy waned every afternoon. On top of these things, I knew the health cards were stacked against me: I had potentially debilitating arthritis and had taken anti-inflammatory drugs every day for twenty years and likely would for the rest of my life, with the risk of severe side effects increasing with the length of use. I thought I should do what I could to keep this body, a gift of God, healthy.

So I started walking a few miles each day. I changed my diet following Michael Pollan's advice: "Eat food. Not too much. Mostly plants."[8] I reduced my caffeine, sugar, and alcohol consumption. In a few months, I felt better than I had at any time I could remember. My energy lasted throughout the day. I slept well at night. My mind seemed sharper, and my jokes got funnier, though some in my household would dispute that last fact.

That is why my spirits sank a few months ago when the pain and stiffness of my arthritis migrated to new places—my upper back, neck, shoulders, jaw, and pinky finger. I began my old habit of catastrophizing, imagining myself in a wheelchair in a decade or unable to drive because I couldn't turn my head. I had taken what control I could of my physical well-being, and this out-of-control disease was still having its way with me. I was impatient to feel good again.

> **TRY THIS:** Over the next five days, keep a record of times when you feel out of control. Later, review your notes prayerfully, imagining ways God might have been present and inviting your patience in those situations.

Fortunately, the moments of near despair, of perseverating and catastrophizing, were companioned by other moments when God gently reminded me to remain open to God's sustaining presence. Moments when, though I was impatient with my own body and unable to control the progression of a disease, God kept speaking to me, teaching me, wooing and loving me.

In other words, God was still answering the prayers of healing prayed for me at that retreat a few years earlier, not that the pain would disappear but that through it the Spirit might continue to transform me in love.

I've begun to sympathize with impatient Peter. After Jesus asked Peter three times whether Peter loved him (I can just hear Peter mumbling, *Can we get on with it please!? I've said yes already!*), Jesus foretold the way Peter was going to die. Jesus also said much about life in general: "[W]hen you were younger, you used to fasten your own belt and to go wherever you wished. But when you grow old, you will stretch out your hands, and someone else will fasten a belt around you and take you where you do not wish to go" (John 21:18). I'm sure this gave Peter much to ponder; I hope he wasn't prone to catastrophizing.

And yet Jesus' words don't portend catastrophe when taken as a statement about life in general. They simply name a reality: A lot of life is done to us. We are not in control. Anyone who has survived the parental strictures of adolescence, struggled with a disease, worked under a supervisor, or suffered the losses that come with aging knows this to be true. We live with illusions that we are rulers of the realms of our own lives. But from the moment our feet hit the floor in the morning, people, culture, nature, and chance begin to exert their pressure on us, and by the end of the day we wonder, *How did I get here?*

One possible approach to this reality is to emerge from the bedroom each morning armed for a great battle, to struggle for control of every minute of every day. We can approach life that way and no doubt win some small, fleeting victories. But do we really want to hack our way through the precious hours of our days, shields raised and swords drawn?

The other approach—patient willingness—receives each moment as it is, knowing that God's grace frees us to respond creatively as we participate with God in shaping for the better the hours we are given.

We don't control our life with God either. Fortunately, God is good, if sometimes more mysterious than we'd prefer. Still, the God revealed in Jesus Christ is trustworthy. In God's hands we can shed our impatience, release our illusions, and allow ourselves to follow wherever the Spirit leads us. Trusting that this leading is for our good. Believing the Spirit is working in love. Knowing that in us and through us God is finishing a new creation.

However long it might take.

Spiritual Exercises

Sacred Reading

Psalm 40; John 18:1-11; Acts 1: 1-11
(See directions for sacred reading on page 155.)

Practicing Awareness

Take fifteen minutes and, in a spirit of prayer and with an attitude of openness to God, use these questions to look over yesterday or last week:

- When did I notice myself feeling impatient, in a hurry, or out of control during this time? What was that like? How did I act in those situations?
- When did I sense God's presence or love during those times of feeling impatient?
- When did I notice myself feeling at ease with times when I was not in control or things were not going as I had planned? What was that like? How did I act in those situations?
- When during this time did I approach life *willfully?*
- When during this time did I approach life *willingly?*
- What am I learning about myself and God's work in my life as I consider these questions? What is God teaching me? How will I respond?

Close with prayer, giving thanks for what God has shown you and asking God to help you to be more aware of and responsive to God's loving agency in your life.

Prompts for Journaling

Write a letter to God, sharing with God how frustrating it is to feel out of control. Be as honest as you can. If you desire it, ask God in your own words to help you live with the patience of being out of control, whatever that means to you. Don't be afraid to plead with God for an end to violence, injustice, and hate, while asking God for the grace to be patient with God's mysterious ways.

Now, write a letter to yourself *from* God. How do you imagine God would respond to the letter you wrote to God?

5

Dropping Our Seriousness

Playfulness

We are afraid to let our souls play. We are cautious lest we
be taken for fools. . . . Stop riding the brakes on the heart.

—Samuel H. Miller, *The Life of the Soul*

I came across as serious and focused. At least that's how a friend in seminary
told me my classmates viewed me. Actually, it was worse: They thought I
was aloof and condescending. I had no idea—so maybe add "out of touch."
"You walked through the hallways so fast," he said. "You were so focused,
like you didn't have the time—or didn't care enough—to stop and talk to
the rest of us. You were stuck up, we thought. Too good for the rest of us."
I was shocked when he told me this, though I recognized his description
of how I motored through the hallways. In reality I was stressed and in my
head, my anxiety and introversion masquerading as disregard. I was not so
much condescending as oblivious.

I felt especially this way—in my head and anxious—when the pressure
was on, as it was a few years later when I was pastoring a small, declining
congregation in rural North Carolina and felt the need to succeed as a pastor at the same time I was trying to figure out how to father two toddler

boys and finish a doctoral dissertation. Add to that the stress of making sure I didn't slip off anyone's radar screen as I toiled away in a church six miles outside of the county seat of nowhere.

Fortunately, I had a spiritual director at the time. His office was a place where the pressure, stress, and fear of being forgotten could rise to my lips, spill out into the clear air, and be seen in the light of grace.

But often we never got to that stuff. I would start our conversation with a story about playing with my boys. A story about tossing and chasing a huge beach ball with them in the wide field between our house and the church. A story about wrestling with them on the family room floor. A story about hiding behind furniture and launching balled-up socks as two toddler boys dove for cover. Often, to my surprise, the hour would pass, and we would never have discussed the more traditionally "spiritual" stuff. And I would find myself in tears because I had been given the gift of insight, the gift to glimpse the Spirit at play in our play, to grasp that grace was frolicking and tumbling right along with us. In us. Through us.

I think my spiritual director knew that this serious young man—husband, father, pastor, PhD in the making—needed to learn that we can be open to God in every aspect of our lives. That life with God isn't just the serious parts. He knew I would learn that the spiritual life is not just a part of life but is all of life, the whole thing, including beach balls and tossed socks and carpet burns acquired in well-worth-it wrestling matches.

He knew God had something to teach me: that playfulness is one aspect of a contemplative approach to life with God. He knew it was the posture I most needed to learn. He knew Jesus was speaking to *me* when Jesus said that to enter God's kingdom you must become like a little child. I suspect I'm not alone.

The Freedom of Playfulness

"My problem," writes Belden Lane, a scholar of Christian mysticism, "is one of limited imagination. Like most of us, I simply can't believe that God's love is actually as exuberant and playful as it is."[1]

I believe he's right. Why is this truth so hard to imagine?

Lane's admission of a failure to imagine God's own playfulness likely indicates the rigidity of our usual approach to life. A rigid, non-playful posture approaches the world as fixed. It can't imagine things any other way. It looks at God and life through a frozen frame. It can't understand the famous line of the Zen master Shunryu Suzuki: "In the beginner's mind there are many possibilities; in the expert's mind there are few."[2]

Playfulness says to allow yourself the freedom of the beginner.

Psychologists call this rigid view of life "functional fixedness." That term names the difficulty some people have imagining a use for an object other than the use it was designed for. I remember one of the most important rules in my grandmother's house when I was a child: "Beds are for lying on; chairs are for sitting on." She would say this if she caught us with our bottoms on the edge of a bed. Sitting on a bed simply wasn't allowed— not to pull on a pair of jeans, not to tie a pair of sneakers. Someone with functional fixedness can't imagine swatting a spider with a broom, can't countenance playing music with wine glasses, can't abide using a coffee-table book as a lap desk. *Books are for reading!*

After my mother died, I ended up with her recipe box, a battered cardboard thing held together by yellowing nylon tape. Not long ago, I was rifling through the box looking for her apple pie recipe. The card wasn't tucked in the dessert section, so I sought it among the side dishes and salads elsewhere in the box. While searching for it, I discovered a photocopy of someone's typed list of unexpected uses for a product called Avon Skin-So-Soft, a bath oil my mother used in the eighties. Apparently the product removes "soap scum from shower doors, shower curtains, windows, and bathroom and kitchen fixtures" and "scuff marks from patent leather shoes" and, my favorite as a father of three children, "chewing gum from hair, skin, and most non-porous surfaces."

As I read the list, I wondered what kind of person wakes up in the morning and says, "Today I'm going to rub a bath oil on my shoes; maybe it will remove those darn scuffs." Whoever it was, I bet it would be fun to spend a Friday evening with them—so few constraints on their imagination, on their willingness to give-it-a-try, on their ability to see endless possibilities in the moment and in the mundane. Someone with functional fixedness—which is each of us to a degree—would be appalled by this list. *But that's not what it's for!* Most people see a bath oil and think to use it only as a bath oil. A blessed few see limitless potential.

> **CONSIDER THIS:**
> What does the saying about beginner's mind mean to you? Do you approach life that way?

Jesus never tells us what he means when he says that we must become like little children to enter the kingdom of God, so I like to imagine that his fondness for childhood stems from the unconstrained, playful nature of a child's imagination, the way a child can spy possibility in the unlikeliest of places—a trait necessary, it seems to me, to see the hidden reality of God's kingdom lurking where most of us would never dare to look. An imagination that can see a sword in a stick, a rocket ship in a refrigerator box, or an ocean in a mud puddle is the kind of imagination that

> **CONSIDER THIS:**
> Imagine that you are again a child at play. Can you remember what that felt like? How often do you still get to experience the freedom of play?

can see a feast in a few loaves of bread or the face of Christ in those who are poor, naked, and imprisoned.

It's as if Jesus were saying, "In the child's mind there are many possibilities, but in the grown-up's there are few." To see and enter God's kingdom we need the former.

Playfulness makes up part of a contemplative posture toward life, open to divine possibilities, able to see new avenues in what look like dead ends, able to find seeds of hope in a barren desert. This approach may seem insignificant when it's about sitting on the edge of beds or imaging that a broom could be a motorcycle. But what about when it comes to working with a child who's been labeled "troubled"? What about when an annoying coworker walks into your office? What about when we encounter—or join the ranks of—the people society has taught us to see as lazy and worthless? Cultural scripts and stereotypes—ideologies and racist conditioning—can freeze our imaginations and cause us to view people in shallow, one-dimensional ways. Fixed ways. When we relate to them accordingly, we perpetuate injustice and inequity. A playful posture helps us to break free from these damaging constraints. A playful posture says that nothing is determined. A playful posture recognizes that each person is more than what our experience of them so far leads us to believe or what the cultural scripts we've internalized tell us about them. The curiosity of playfulness looks for more, waits for the surprise.

> **TRY THIS:** Watch children play. What do you notice? Could what you see become a metaphor for your life with God?

89

Patron Saint of Playfulness

The ability to imagine the divine possibilities in a person or a particular circumstance is characteristic of many of the people we've come to know as Saints with a capital "S." Perhaps none more so than St. Francis, the medieval saint whose likeness stands in so many flower gardens. As one born into privilege, Francis's vision of the world was narrow and constrained. According to Jon M. Sweeney, a recent biographer of Francis's, "In 1204, at the age of twenty-three, Francis was still his father's son, unconsciously pursuing what his father valued: reputation, status, and wealth."[3] Francis was living with an inherited view of what matters in life and wasn't even aware of it. This pursuit led him to a humiliating attempt to prove himself in battle. Francis set off for battle hoping to secure that reputation and status. He returned humbled, tail between his legs.

But that defeat led to liberation. What Gerald May said of the spiritual life in general applies to St. Francis's humiliation: "When the spiritual life feels so uprooted, it can be almost impossible to believe—or even to consider—that what's really going on is a graceful process of liberation, a letting go of old, limiting habits to make room for a fresh openness to love."[4] When our rigid, constrained ways of being in the world are being jostled free by grace, and it hurts for a while, it's hard to believe that what's really going on is the birth of a playful, free spirit, newly open to the possibilities of love.

These are the birth pangs of an everyday contemplative.

They certainly were for Francis. A crushing blow to his ego also smashed the rigidity of his aspirations. Now he aspired to see and live in the world through God's imagination, which led people of his time to dub him and the men who associated with him "God's *jongleurs.*" Sweeney notes, "A *jongleur* was a troubadour—which also sometimes meant that he was an acrobat, fiddler, dancer, and poet."[5] Francis approached life and God with a playful spirit. In *When Saint Francis Saved the Church*, Sweeney shows how Francis's playfulness allowed him to invent a revolutionary spirituality. Francis improvised his way into a new understanding of friendship; he saw beauty and grace in those who were marginalized and outcast like people with leprosy; he embodied radical connection with the rest of God's creation, seeing all creatures as part of God's family; and he approached death without fear in a culture that said death, above all else, should be feared. "His welcoming of death was almost without precedent in Christian teaching."[6]

> **TRY THIS:** Make a list of people you know who have a playful, open, and curious approach to life. What about them allows them to live this way?

He saw possibility where other thirteenth-century eyes could see only impossibilities. Indeed, where many twenty-first century eyes would only see impossibilities.

All of this was because, by God's grace, he traded the bedazzled robes of a rigid outlook for the bedraggled garments of playfulness.

All because his new playfulness left him open, available, and responsive to God.

Play As an End in Itself

When I was a pastor, we sometimes planned worship services around themes that would allow us to be more playful in worship, to drop our seriousness next to the umbrella stand in the narthex and enter the sanctuary with lighter spirits. One Sunday we dubbed the service "Sunday at the Beach" because I was planning to preach on Jesus' feeding the disciples fish on the shoreline after the resurrection. Congregants dressed in shorts and Hawaiian shirts. Beach balls bounced around the sanctuary. Seashells dotted the altar rail. The mood was relaxed, like we were on vacation. Another Sunday I preached on the story in Genesis of Jacob sleeping out in the middle of nowhere with a rock for a pillow after fleeing his angry brother Esau. We called the service "Under the Stars" and decorated the sanctuary with a camping theme. A tent stood next to the pulpit. Silver stars dangled on fishing line from the choir loft and the balcony. Sleeping bags stretched unfurled up front. Nothing about worship said we couldn't have a little fun.

Looking back now on those Sundays when we invited playfulness into our worship space, I see we were highlighting a characteristic of all worship. We were foregrounding a key aspect of worship, for worship and play have something very much in common.

What that commonality is, Alasdair MacIntyre, one of the most influential moral philosophers of the last forty years, makes clear in a different context entirely. MacIntyre's philosophy of virtue hinges on his idea of a *practice*, an activity people do together over time that has—and here's the key phrase—"goods internal to that form of activity."[7] That's philosopher speak for a practice we engage in for its own sake. The practice contains its own rewards.

MacIntyre offers chess as an example.[8] If you are teaching two children how to play chess, you want them to discover the intrinsic joys of the game, the "goods" that come with playing the game. That should be motivation enough to play. But you could also bribe them to play by promising them candy after they finish each game. The candy is *not* a good internal to the game. If the kids play chess for the candy, they're playing for a reason other than chess itself. In fact, they might never discover the joy that comes with the game because they are only thinking about the reward. Introducing an external good—a reward—corrupts the game because playing the game should be its own reward.

Similarly, worship is an end in itself.

Think of that kid Jesus invited onto his knee, the one we must be like if we want to crawl into God's kingdom. I bet she was impatient sitting there. What kid wants to be an object lesson? Especially when she can see her friends—her playmates—in the empty field a hundred yards away, swatting at rocks with a stick and can imagine herself out there—lost in the game, abandoning herself to the moment, to the activity, all externals slipping away.

Could that be the very quality of childhood playfulness Jesus was pointing us toward?

What's true in play and in worship—that both are ends in themselves —is true in life with God: We live a life open to God for its own sake. Like true play, open availability to God *doesn't accomplish anything.* This is a countercultural notion, and it's not a little challenging.

I see that challenge in my students. I teach introduction to spirituality at a seminary, and I introduce my students to many practices of prayer, requiring them to give each one a try. I remind them of the pithy advice of Dom John Chapman, a Benedictine abbot from the early twentieth century: "Pray as you can, do not try to pray as you can't."[9] But I also ask them how they could know which ways they can and can't pray if they don't experiment.

Many of my students consider contemplative silence one of the ways they *can't*—and not only because of distracting thoughts. Students report that sitting for ten or fifteen minutes in silence and not doing anything—a candle burning next to them, their hands folded gently in their laps, their attention resting on their breathing or the repetition of a sacred word, and a paper not getting written and dishes not getting washed and bills not getting paid—makes them feel like they are wasting their time. *How can we justify just sitting when there's so much to do?*

Sitting in silence with God has this countercultural drawback: It doesn't get anything done.

> **CONSIDER THIS:** What do you think about the idea that prayer doesn't accomplish anything but is more like wasting time with God? How difficult is it for you to pray and do nothing else?

Now, I could tell my students they are perhaps lowering their blood pressure or calming their anxiety or recharging their batteries so they can work more efficiently after the minutes of silence, but that would be like offering candy to the kids playing chess. If we live in a genuinely make-something-happen-culture, as I suggested in the first chapter, then the playfulness of life with God can seem like an irrelevance at best and a stumbling block at worst because it doesn't achieve anything.

Which is exactly why we need it.

We were made for life with God, but North American culture teaches us that we were made to identify and accomplish objectives. A well-lived human life should have a sense of purpose; we do have an internal drive to make a meaningful contribution to society. But absent a sense of our truest purpose, which is to enjoy God, the pursuit of reward and achievement and accomplishment becomes an idolatrous substitute, and we live less than fully human lives.

Recovering a sense of playfulness in worship, prayer, and life can reorder things and put our other pursuits in proper perspective. It can help us to be open to the useless beauty of life. It can restore a sense of the intrinsic worth of our own being, outside of anything we can accomplish. It can help us relearn that, in God's eyes, we are ends in ourselves. God simply enjoys us for who we are, not for what we can do for God. Rediscovering prayer and life as a kind of play can help us enter—and enjoy—this liberating truth.

Approaching Prayer Playfully

These two insights about playfulness—that playfulness overcomes a fixed perspective, allowing for multiple grace-filled possibilities, and that playfulness helps us to approach life with God as an end in itself—can shape our approach to prayer, those times we have reserved for giving our full attention to being open, available, and responsive to God.

Many of us learned to pray according to certain rules or patterns. Some of us learned the acronym ACTS—Adoration, Confession, Thanksgiving, and Supplication—and were told that genuine prayer must include each of these. When I'm leading a retreat and introduce prayer as listening to God, folks who have learned that ACTS is the right way to pray get fidgety. I can see the resistance in their eyes. After the teaching session, I send the group into the silence to take a walk in the woods, pace peacefully through a labyrinth, or sit quietly in the sun—to do anything that will help them quiet their hearts and adopt a listening posture toward God. There are always a few people who linger around after the presentation, not sure what to do. Or they open their laptops to check their email or head back to their rooms to nap—each a form of resistance. Later during the time of sharing, I will learn that they rejected my invitation to listen because it felt to them like I was asking them to betray the way they were taught to pray. Somehow, they would be dishonoring their former youth leaders or their parents if their prayer colored outside of the lines.

> **CONSIDER THIS:** Do you prefer to have strict guidelines for prayer or a more flexible structure? Why?

When I have bona fide rule-followers in a group, they often want to follow *my* rules. If I'm introducing a way of prayer that seems to have steps—like *lectio divina*, with its four phases of reading scripture, meditating on scripture, praying to God, and contemplating God in stillness—they will trip all over themselves trying to do it the *right* way. They'll be so focused on following the rules, they'll miss the Spirit of God just waiting to surprise them. They come back from the time of silence frustrated because they were paralyzed by fear of doing it wrong.

We need to remember one thing: The rules serve the pray-er; the pray-er doesn't serve the rules. The *point* of the guidelines is to help us become increasingly open to God, not to do it right. Prayer is an end in itself. The rules aren't. A playful approach appreciates this.

My mom taught me how to swing dance in our family room when I was about ten, and I stumbled through the basic steps, eyes always glued to my feet: *left-together, right-together, back-together; left-together.* By the time I got married when I was twenty-six, my wife and I danced our first dance at the reception to "In the Mood," saxophones and trumpets accompanying our spinning around the fellowship hall. She twirled; I ducked. She slid past me; I pulled her back. She spun beneath my arched armed; I reciprocated. Somewhere in our dancing those basic steps were present— *left-together, right-together, back-together*—but we weren't slaves to them. Having internalized these "rules," we were able to improvise. The dance was ours, and it was fun. We forgot that two hundred other people were in the room watching.

I tell people who are worried about following the rules—for whom a certain way of prayer feels like breaking the law or for whom following the guidelines perfectly becomes paramount—that learning prayer can feel awkward at first. Being patient with that awkwardness matters. There's no shame in pausing to look at a book or a handout that lists guidelines or steps to remind yourself where you are in the process.

But I suggest combining a respect for the usefulness of guidelines with permission to be playful. The guidelines for the practice of praying with scripture called *lectio divina,* for instance, usually suggest reading the scripture passage all the way through four times. But if God captures your attention the first time through with a word or phrase or image, it's fine simply to pause and hang out with God right there. That honors the intent of the prayer practice, which is what the guidelines are meant to help you do anyway. Were you open and available to God and able to respond to God's presence to you through scripture? *Okay then.*

We want to get on with things, to accomplish something, to do it right. But we give ourselves a great gift if we give ourselves permission to play when we sit down to pray. Tell yourself there's no right way to do this. You might have to say it a hundred times for a hundred days before you believe it: *There's no right way to do this.* Say to yourself: *This time of prayer doesn't have to accomplish anything.* Remind yourself as often as you need to: *I'm not trying to accomplish something here.* Say to yourself: *It's okay for this to be fun.* Prayer won't always be fun; sometimes it will be dry or confusing or boring. But having fun doesn't mean you've done it wrong.

You can enjoy prayer. You can enjoy God in prayer. Full stop.

Let the pages of the Bible flop open on your lap, or hold the beads gently in your grasp, or spread the mandala and colored pencils on the desk in front of you—or do whatever you do that you consider prayer—and, with childlike wonder, imagination, and sense of play, *begin.*

> **TRY THIS:**
> Go play!

Don't be too shocked if the God of surprises has something unexpected in store for you.

Spiritual Exercises

Sacred Reading

Psalm 104:1-26; Psalm 150; Mark 10:13-16
(See directions for sacred reading on page 155.)

Practicing Awareness

Over the next week, pay attention to the possibility of approaching life with a beginner's mind—with a playful, curious spirit. Approach your times of prayer this way as well. At the end of the week, take some time to look over the week in prayer, using these questions as a guide:

- When did I notice a playful, curious spirit within myself?
- What difference did that spirit make in my daily interactions?
- When did I notice myself resisting being playful and relaxed, but opting instead for being more rigid? What difference did that make in my daily interactions?
- How did approaching life playfully help me be more aware of God's grace and presence in my life?
- How did approaching life with a playful attitude help me be more responsive to God's grace and presence in my life?

Close with prayer, giving thanks for what God has shown you and asking God to help you be more aware of and responsive to God's loving agency in your life.

Prompts for Journaling

Write a letter to God about how the idea of approaching prayer and life with God playfully feels inviting or challenging to you. Be as honest as you can. Tell God where you see this need for a playful, relaxed spirit in your life. Ask God for the freedom you need to live with a beginner's mind. Share with God anything else you need to about your hopes and fears related to living more playfully.

Now, write a letter to yourself *from* God. How do you imagine God would respond to the letter you wrote to God?

6

Lowering Our Defenses

Vulnerability

I love; therefore I am vulnerable.

—MADELEINE L'ENGLE, *WALKING ON WATER*

It's 8:25 in the morning on a Wednesday. Students are shuffling into room 216 for their first morning class. Some carry mugs of coffee. One wears a hoodie, drawstring pulled tight around his face as if he's not yet ready to face the world—or for it to face him. Nine students in all take their place around tables arranged in a rectangle at one end of the room, the end with the audio-visual equipment, podium for the teacher, and new chalk in the tray beneath the green chalkboard. We've started calling this the academic end of the room. The end where I give mini-lectures and we discuss common readings. The end where we dialogue and disagree and debate.

But it's a long room, and at the other end things look different. At the other end ten chairs are arranged in the circle I described in chapter 3. There is a cloth-draped coffee table in the middle on which sits a battery-powered candle and three crosses—a simple wooden one, a brass one, and one bearing an icon of Jesus, the famous San Damiano crucifix. At this end we don't debate. Here we practice awareness. We breathe, we sit in silence, we sing, we pray.

Here we speak. Here we listen. That's what you do in a spiritual formation class.

Here we practice vulnerability so we can be better at being vulnerable at the other end of the room and when we leave the room to face the world—and for it to face us.

It's not easy, this vulnerability. Parker Palmer says, "The soul is like a wild animal—tough, resilient, savvy, self-sufficient, and yet exceedingly shy."[1] He reminds us that we must become still and quiet to see a wild animal; it won't show itself unless it feels safe. The same is true of the soul. I tell my students what Palmer says, promising that I will bear responsibility for keeping our time in the circle safe so that they can feel free to speak. I will make sure we observe the ground rules (confidentiality; silence after sharing; no correcting or arguing or judging; honest listening) and remind them that they are completely free to speak or not speak when it's time to share—time to speak about our own lives of prayer, what we're noticing God is up to in our lives, how we are struggling, or what we are hoping for. There is no coercion in the circle.

I also tell them that, though I intend to keep the circle a safe space for their shy souls to show themselves, I can't guarantee it won't be challenging or that they won't hear others say things they disagree with or that trigger painful emotions in them. Even in a controlled environment like the circle at the end of room 216, there is risk in letting our defenses down, risk in offering our lives authentically, risk in receiving the offering of others.

Indeed, there is risk in opening our lives to this God who transforms us. Transforming sometimes means seeing things about ourselves we didn't want to see and changing in ways we never would have imagined.

That's why we practice. Dropping our defenses and being vulnerable is necessary for being open to the gift of God in our lives. And to the gift of others as well.

It's part of the posture of an everyday contemplative.

Defended

Two questions in David Whyte's poem "Self-Portrait" haunt me. One asks if we are ready to live with the world's attempts to change us. The other asks if we can live every day with love's consequences.[2] Until reading this poem, I had never considered those two realities so clearly: that the people who surround us and the institutions we inhabit need to fashion us in their image rather than leave us as we are, and that choosing love means risking consequences like having our love rejected or being rejected by others because of the commitments toward which love calls us.

In other words, this poem is asking if we can risk vulnerability. I suspect the answer is often no—because we know too much. We know how much it hurts for the world to try to change us, how much sting there can be in love's ramifications. We're not surprised that the word *vulnerable* comes from a Latin noun that means "wound." Why would we open ourselves to being wounded? Why would we expose ourselves to the world's arrows?

As I observe the lives of others from the perspective of pastor, professor, and friend, and as I look at my own life, I see three prominent defense strategies to deflect the world's attempts to change us and to forestall love's painful consequences.

The first strategy is *religiosity*. We believe if we just practice our faith the right way we will make it through the world unscathed. If we do our devotions, go to church, sing in the choir, and serve on the finance committee, we will prove to others (and to God?) that we are worthy. That we matter. As someone who is professionally religious, I know the temptation to allow the appearance of my religiosity be a defense against criticism and a symbol of my worth. Though most people don't get to wear the fancy robes and stoles of the ordained, anyone can wear their religious devotion as a defense. Jesus warned against this kind of false religiosity in the Sermon on the Mount when he said, "And whenever you pray, do not be like the hypocrites; for they love to stand and pray in the synagogues and at the street corners, so that they may be seen by others" (Matt. 6:5). Even though church affiliation is carrying less and less cachet in many places, we can still be rewarded by recognition in our own religious communities. And we can believe this recognition will somehow protect us.

The second strategy is *expertise.* One way we believe we can secure our place in a world that wants to change us is by becoming good at something—really good. Like religiosity, expertise brings recognition; it becomes the foundation on which we imagine we can build a stable identity establishing our place in the world. Experts are *needed.* Finally, someone will tell us how great we are—a parent who always ignored us perhaps or the internalized voice of the judging parent within. People will no longer be able to deny that we matter. Just think of a doctor's office wallpapered with diplomas and awards. Or a pastor's study with framed diplomas and certificates on the wall. Are they to assure the parishioners who visit for advice that the pastor knows what they're doing, or are they for the pastor's own comfort—to remind them that they're competent and have a reason for being there?

The final strategy is *success.* We can wear success as a sturdy mask to defend us from the onslaught of a world that judges people by their accomplishments. As an academic, I know the power of a twelve-page CV with its list of peer-reviewed articles, books published by the right presses, conference presentations, and invited lectures. I know how it often feels like success is a limited commodity—there doesn't seem to be enough to go around. As a parent, I know the pressure I put on my children to succeed and how quick they are to tell me when they do—when they win that debate tournament, make the All-State Choir, or ace a vocabulary quiz. They have learned success is the currency that can purchase acceptance in the right places.

I'm certain an astute observer of human nature could list many other defense strategies, such as the accumulation of resources, the development of rugged independence, and the simplification of life. What these strategies share is the way they become like a shell that protects the shy soul—the true authentic self—from the fear that it's not enough *on its own*—not good, gifted, or beautiful enough—to truly belong in the world. They protect the true authentic self that fears it is not resilient enough to withstand the wounding words and actions of the people whose acceptance it so desires.

We become like a medieval knight. We wear a helmet and a suit of armor so the world can't get to us and see us for what we really are. But at what cost do we wear these defenses? At the cost of knowing the gift that we truly are or of experiencing the healing grace of divine love? At the cost of allowing ourselves to share that healing grace with others?

These defense strategies have one other thing in common: They are bound to fail.

One Side of Vulnerability: Offering Our Truest Selves

If these strategies are going to fail, why not set them aside willingly? Why wait until circumstances conspire against us and we are left humiliated and humbled? Why not adopt a posture of vulnerability as we seek to be contemplatively open to God in our praying and living? An everyday contemplative simply can't wear pads and a mask and a helmet. Something will tear them off. Why not let that something be *us*?

But what does a vulnerable posture toward life, prayer, and God look like? Such a posture, it seems to me, has two related sides, the first of which is *offering*.

As I write this, the Christian calendar tells me today is Epiphany. The scripture passage I read for meditation this morning spoke of wise men from the east who followed a star and journeyed long and far to reach a baby who, they learned, would be king of the Jews (see Matthew 2:2). It also told of an earthly king who felt threatened by this child and lied to the wise men so that he could find the child and murder him. And though this treacherous king didn't kill his target, the wise men still gave the child myrrh, a gift symbolic of death. As we sing in the hymn "We Three Kings," this gift of myrrh "breathes a life of gathering gloom; sorrowing, sighing, bleeding, dying, sealed in a stone-cold tomb."[3]

Epiphany shows us that God appears in the world as a dependent, vulnerable child, threatened from birth and destined to suffer—because that's what happens when you live a fully human life of vulnerable love. When you choose to put away your defenses.

God shows up in Christ as a vulnerable God. As theologian William C. Placher writes, "Trust in such a God can give human beings the strength to risk following on the path of compassion and vulnerability, to think what it means to live lives whose first priority is love."[4]

Human beings: That's us.

The gifts of God's vulnerable presence and love make it possible for us to offer our lives to God and others. To show up in the world risking love. To show up as our truest selves. To show up to prayer that way. To show up to work that way. To show up among friends and family that way.

Remember what Thomas Merton wrote: "For me to be a saint means to be myself."[5] The journey to *myself* is often long and vulnerable.

Offering ourselves in authentic vulnerable love is not easy. Don't think it's something you can do immediately, like Clark Kent hopping into a phone booth and emerging as Superman. We naturally want to feel safe and affirmed in our lives, and we know there are places where that's not possible. So sometimes, on the way to approaching life with increasing vulnerability, we need to cultivate spaces where we know we are wanted, loved, and affirmed as who we are.

Do you have a spiritual director or soul friend in whose presence you can drop the mask—someone who won't judge or condemn you, but in whose presence you practice showing your truest self in the world? According to Edward Sellner, an expert on Celtic spirituality, "Soul friendship is a relationship that acts as a container, a cell in which we can face the truth of our lives without fear. Soul friendship is a place of sanctuary where the worst part of us can be acknowledged, so that genuine change can begin to occur. Soul friendship is also a relationship, a place where our joys and accomplishments can be celebrated wholeheartedly."[6]

> **CONSIDER THIS:**
> Where are the places in your life right now where you can offer your true self and be fully known? How does it feel to be in those spaces?

I don't know of anyone who doesn't need such a holy container. As we learn to approach life vulnerably in these spaces, our courage grows; we begin to feel able to risk offering our truest selves in more and more spaces in our lives. Maybe that container is created for us by a spiritual director, a spouse, a dear soul friend, or a small group. However we find it, there can be no doubt that it is a necessary for living with a posture of vulnerability.

We need to practice courageous vulnerability within the safe container created by people who love us, because sometimes we might find ourselves called to vulnerable speech in a public way where the risks are higher. The prophet Nathan must have felt vulnerable when he confronted King David about raping Bathsheba and murdering Uriah. John the Baptist was beheaded after he confronted Herod about an immoral relationship. They both "spoke truth to power"—and there were no guarantees how it would turn out. There still aren't. But courageous Christians through the centuries have been willing to speak when they've witnessed injustices and oppression.

> **CONSIDER THIS:** Are there relationships in your life right now where you feel like you need to speak your truth? What's holding you back? How about your relationship with God?

Sometimes it's hard to be vulnerable with God as well; we feel we need to protect God from our deepest feelings, especially if they are of doubt, fear, or anger. But the Bible gives remarkable examples of faithful people showing God their most authentic selves. The Psalms are full of instances of God's people speaking honestly to God, offering themselves in anger, frustration, and confession. Surely that kind of honest, vulnerable offering was key to their remaining open, available, and responsive to God.

The Other Side of Vulnerability: Receiving

If one side of the coin of vulnerability involves offering our truest selves in the world, the other side of the coin is stamped *receiving*. Vulnerability includes openness to receive the pain of others, the wisdom and warning of friends, and the truth God wants us to see about ourselves.

Before I visit my spiritual director, Sr. Anna, I review what I've written in my journal in the previous month and make some notes about what I want to talk about. I know that her office is a place I can make an offering of myself and let my shy soul peek out from behind any one of the many masks it often wears.

We start by sitting in silence, then one of us voices a prayer, and then I start talking.

Before the hour is over, I'm reminded of what Margaret Guenther, one of the foremost writers on the spiritual life in recent decades, used to say to people who came to her for spiritual direction. She would clap her hands together in gleeful anticipation and say, "Let's have a holy chat." *Chat*. She didn't say, "I'm here to listen to your holy monologue."[7] Life and prayer are chats, conversations—give and take—rather than monologues. Narcissists believe all that matters is what they say, what they feel, how they see the world. But those hoping to live open to God in each moment know that life is a conversation—there is offering and there is receiving.

Sr. Anna will definitely have something to say, and that means I will have something to receive. Sometimes it will be affirmation, sometimes suggestion. Sometimes she will ask a probing question that implies I might be off track or that there's something I'm missing.

I don't like probing questions. *Can't we stick with affirmation?*

But when I return to her office a month later, having taken time to chew on her question and let it bounce around in my mind and rattle around in my soul, I invariably say something like, "Now that I've had time to sit with it, that question you asked (which I didn't like in the moment) has become really helpful." It might take a month, but eventually I'm able to receive.

Prayer is the same way. In prayer there's both speaking and listening, offering and receiving. When I teach a session on prayer at a church or on a retreat and talk about prayer as listening—not just speaking—to God, there are always some in the crowd who have never considered this possibility. I remember one Wednesday evening I was teaching *lectio divina*—the spiritual reading of scripture—as a way to hear what God wants to speak into our lives at that moment. After the practice ended, a man about my age and a faithful church attender his whole life, said to the group, "I think that's the first time in my life I've ever heard God speak to me through scripture."

> **TRY THIS:** Draw a picture of what a posture of receiving means to you. You can draw anything (no rules!). Put this picture somewhere you'll see it as a reminder to be open to receive from God and others.

It's never too late to start receiving.

Life is always throwing something at us, insults and blessings, criticism and praise. Some of what we receive is justified; some is bunk. But in all of it, through the mysteries of God's grace, God is present, inviting us to a deeper realization of who we truly are and who this God who walks with us throughout our days truly is.

Receiving the Wisdom of Jesus

Theologian William C. Placher asks what kind of God we would believe in if we "took the biblical narratives, especially the Gospel stories about Jesus, as the best clue to who God is." He answers his own question: "God is the one who loves in freedom, and in that free love God is vulnerable, willing to risk suffering."[8] In the stories of Jesus, we discover God's identity as the one offering self in vulnerable love and willing to receive the consequences of that love. So it should be no surprise then that Jesus has something to teach us about a posture of vulnerability.

Over the years, as I've read and prayed through the Gospels, three of Jesus' sayings have struck me as offering guidance on embracing vulnerability. If God's word, as one psalm says, is a lamp to our feet and a light to our path (see Psalm 119:105), then these words of Jesus shine like a flashlight on the path to a vulnerable life.

"Let your word be 'Yes, yes' or 'No, no'; anything more than this comes from the evil one." (Matt. 5:37)

Authentic, vulnerable lives avoid equivocation, prevarication, and all manner of obfuscation. In other words, they embrace clear, direct speech. So often we obscure our true selves behind the mask of language, letting our language become a tool of defense, mechanism for manipulation, or a scrim for hiding behind. Jesus invites us to follow another path and use our language for honest, authentic communication. Jesus knows our false selves are tempted to twist language for their own purposes (maybe that's what he means when he says untruthful speech comes from evil). The opposite—straightforward speech—comes only with graceful practice.

We know language can be used to hide truth rather than reveal it. A politician caught in a scandal stands at a podium surrounded by the symbols of power and announces, "Mistakes were made," instead of telling the truth: "I screwed up." A student turning in a late paper says, "Last week all my classes had papers due at the same time," rather than taking responsibility: "I managed my time poorly." A worn-out mother says, "Sure, I don't mind," when her son asks her to drive him to the store to buy a toy, instead of saying how she feels: "Actually, I'm tired and I'm going to sit and rest." We are tempted daily to string words together that say something other than the truth.

When the pressure is on to hide behind half-truths or say what other people want us to say, Jesus invites vulnerable, straightforward truth-telling: *Let your word be "Yes, yes," or "No, no."*

"Let your light shine before others, so that they may see your good works and give glory to your Father in heaven." (Matt. 5:16)

Every kid in Sunday school has sung "This Little Light of Mine" and had the meaning hammered into them through a million children's sermons: Your life is like a light, and you should let it shine. But as they grow up, the world teaches them something else: You aren't good enough, quick enough, pretty enough, bright enough—you don't really have a light. Or they discover the hard way that letting their light shine will tempt someone to snuff it out.

As a seminary faculty member, I hear the stories of gay and lesbian students who have been told subtly and explicitly by their parents and their congregations that God doesn't want them to shine *their* lights, that the doors of ministry are closed to them. Sometimes I want to weep when I hear their stories of the pain and injustice they've suffered. And I weep with joy when I hear them tell about how someone—a college chaplain perhaps or a non-Christian friend—affirmed their gifts, worth, and humanity. I also hear stories from students of color who have been made to feel their whole lives that they have nothing to offer the world or that the institutions they've been a part of—schools, churches, and workplaces—don't value them as they are but subtly encourage them to act more "white" in order to fit in and succeed. For many of these students, it has felt safer to spend much of their lives hiding.

> **TRY THIS:** Read the Sermon on the Mount (Mathew 5–7) through the lens of vulnerability. Which of Jesus' teachings in these chapters help you understand what it means to live an authentic, vulnerable life?

To them—and to any person who has been made to believe they don't have gifts worth sharing or a life worth offering—Jesus says, "Let it shine! You are a precious light in the world just the way you are." I imagine Jesus inviting them to practice shining their lights in the places that will accept them while they grow the courage to live authentically wherever they are.

> "I do not call you servants any longer, because the servant does not know what the master is doing; but I have called you friends, because I have made known to you everything I have heard from my Father." (John 15:15)

In a small upper room, Jesus shared one of the most vulnerable acts imaginable with his disciples: He washed their feet (see John 13:1-20). Is it any surprise that headstrong Peter would resist this intimacy and what it implies about power—that Jesus' power comes from his willingness to stoop and serve, to make himself vulnerable? This act continued the vulnerability that began when he was a defenseless baby with only a few bands of cloth protecting him from the cruel world. Shortly after this act of foot washing, the very clothes covering Jesus' body would be stripped away, and his body would hang exposed to the cruel world.

In these intimate moments before the crucifixion, Jesus had something to teach about living life open to God in a world that often doesn't care. After the foot washing, Jesus told them he no longer called them servants but friends. Servants live at a distance from the one they serve; they are denied familiarity. But in Jesus, God has invited us into the inner circle of love that is the heart of God's own life. At the same time, God has opened that heart of love to us. We are invited to be friends of God. As true friends of God, God wants us to reveal the hidden recesses of our lives to God, just as in Jesus God pulled back the curtain on God's life for us.

Jesus is affirming that God's own heart is the container in which we can be our truest selves. When others reject us with their words, deny our identity with their actions, or refuse to see the light of our gifts by closing their eyes and turning their backs, God's own life is the home where we can find our truest belonging.

I think of this truth often when I use a popular, Jesuit-designed prayer app I have on my phone.[9] The app leads me through a meditation on a scripture passage, and then a gentle voice with a British accent invites me to "speak to Jesus as to a friend." Ignatius of Loyola, the founder of the Jesuits, spoke this way about prayer, and his spiritual descendants use the same language: Prayer is friendship with Jesus. I find comfort in my praying when I hear those words. When I speak to Jesus as to a friend, nothing needs to remain hidden or unsaid. He takes everything he hears from me—everything he knows of who I am—and holds it in the heart of God.

> **TRY THIS:** The next time you pray, imagine that Jesus is a friend who is visiting and sharing time with you. Speak to Jesus as to a friend. Then reflect on what this was like.

Room 216

When I lecture or preach, people often comment on how vulnerable I appear because I share stories from my own life, especially stories that show I am a learner who still messes up and hasn't quite perfected this task of living. Which puts me in the same category as everyone else in the room. Maybe they're just surprised to hear someone admit it.

On the other hand, I usually have a lectern or pulpit in front of me, and the folks listening are several feet—or yards—away. It's easier to be vulnerable when there's furniture to hide behind and when there's plenty of distance between you and everyone else.

But in the circle in room 216 we practice another way—*I* have to practice another way. I don't get to take my teaching notes with me to the circle. No lectern shields me. There's little distance and only the table, crosses, and candle between us. We are close, and we look one another in the eyes. There, in the circle, I am blessed by the students' sharing, by their vulnerability. When they offer a story about their grief over a parent's death, their own struggle with mental illness, or the acceptance they've finally found as part of an inclusive community, I take courage from their vulnerability.

And when I feel led to share, sometimes I worry because I haven't had a chance to script my contribution. What if I say something wrong, do a bad job saying what I want to say, or begin to get anxious as I speak? What if they see me for the fraud I sometimes feel myself to be? But having taken courage from their vulnerability, I speak, a speaking that I find risky and healing and which I know is giving courage to someone else in the circle, someone who needs to practice offering and receiving in vulnerable love.

In room 216, I experience this truth: There is a mysterious alchemy in offering and receiving, through which all becomes beautiful, becomes grace.

Spiritual Exercises

Sacred Reading

Matthew 5:1-16; John 13:1-17; Psalm 51
(See directions for sacred reading on page 155.)

Practicing Awareness

Take fifteen minutes and, in a spirit of prayer and with an attitude of openness to God, use these questions to look over yesterday or last week:

- When did I have an opportunity to act out of my truest, most authentic self? Did I do it? What was it like?
- When during this period did I feel I needed to hide my truest self or my thoughts and feelings? Why? Looking back, what else could I have done in those moments?
- When has someone made me feel safe, worthy, and valued?
- When have I felt safe, worthy, and valued in God's presence?
- What am I learning about living vulnerably with others and with God from what I am noticing in this time of self-examination?

Close with prayer, giving thanks for what God has shown you and asking God to help you be more aware of and responsive to God's loving agency in your life.

Prompts for Journaling

Write a letter to God about your struggles with vulnerability. Share with God those places in your life where you feel safest to be yourself and those places where you don't feel welcomed to be yourself. Talk with God about what it would take to feel safe and welcome in God's presence. Write this letter to God as if writing to an old, trusted friend.

Now, write a letter to yourself *from* God. How do you imagine God would respond to the letter you wrote to God?

7

Saying Goodbye to Goldilocks

Nonjudgment

Joseph asked [Abba] Poemen, "Tell me how to become a monk." He said, "If you want to find rest in this life and the next, say at every moment, 'Who am I?' and judge no one."

—A SAYING OF THE DESERT FATHERS

I take a walk almost every day. But before I leave, I make calculations about what to wear depending on the weather. I don't want to be too hot or too cold. This is a challenge, given the way the wind whips differently depending on the height of the hill I'm on, the direction I'm treading through a neighborhood, and the prevalence of trees. And I want to stay dry, no easy thing given the unreliability of my weather app. Many times, I begin my walk wearing a cap, a long-sleeved shirt, and a cardigan and end it with my sleeves rolled up, cardigan clutched under my arm, and cap swinging in my hand so my sweaty head can breathe.

I wasn't aware of my efforts to secure my walking comfort until I noticed how judgmental my kids often are about the weather—how they will turn down an invitation to take a walk if it's too hot, too cold, too humid, too sunny, or too overcast. They are the Goldilockses of the daily outing. Fortunately, enough days in the spring and fall are just right that I'm blessed by their company (though there might still be complaints about our speed—one will think our pace too fast, another too slow, and the third just right).

Watching them has helped me see my own habit of judging. Take my walks this fall. When the maple trees burn lava red and the sassafras trees glow a dazzling orange, I could walk for hours, blessed by the beauty of their foliage. But a few weeks later a cold front will pass through, wind gusts will dislodge the leaves, and rain will saturate them on lawns and in gutters. Denuded limbs will stretch to the sky, and a little part of me will grieve as I walk my usual path, especially if I've forgotten to switch from my sweat-stained baseball cap to my wool cap with the earflaps.

There's nothing wrong with having preferences. I prefer it when my back doesn't hurt. I prefer it when the sun shines. I prefer it when the family chooses to get Indian food over McDonald's. But I also know that the habits of judging—labeling each moment "good" or "bad," ranking each moment "better" or "worse," clinging to one moment and rejecting another—can obstruct openness to God in *all* moments and obscure the possibilities of love inherent in each instant of life.

I believe that what Thomas Merton wrote is true and that this truth sits at the heart of being an everyday contemplative:

> For it is God's love that warms me in the sun and God's love that sends the cold rain. It is God's love that feeds me in the bread I eat and God that feeds me also by hunger and fasting. It is the love of God that sends the winter days when I am cold and sick, and the hot summer when I labor and my clothes are full of sweat: but it is God Who breathes on me with light winds off the river and in the breezes out of the wood.[1]

I believe this, but I want to *experience* it—and I know that my habit of hoarding the moments I prefer and rejecting the rest just might foreclose the possibility of being fed by them all.

> **TRY THIS:** Pay attention as you move through the rest of your day to how often you make judgments. How pervasive is this habit?

I hear in Merton's litany an invitation to release judgment and approach prayer, life, and God with a posture of welcome and nonjudgment.

Habits of Judgment

A few moments of attentiveness to our thoughts will reveal for most of us the pervasiveness of our judging, the way we corral every thought or experience toward one side of a binary: us and them, good and bad, pleasant and unpleasant. We render these judgments before we become conscious of them, if we ever do, though they shape our daily interactions in innumerable hidden ways. A posture of nonjudgment helps us to be open and available to the presence of God—to God's grace in every instant and the divine possibilities of every moment. Becoming more aware of the areas of our lives in which judgment occurs, in which our habits of dividing and discriminating reign, will help us move toward a posture of nonjudgment.

Though I'm sure there are more, I can identify three such areas.

We judge other people.

Dietrich Bonhoeffer, a German theologian and church leader executed by the Nazis, was a keen observer of human nature, having lived for a time in an intentional Christian community that was an underground seminary for students preparing for ministry in a church resistant to Nazi ideology and idolatry. In *Life Together,* his book about his experience living with seminarians, Bonhoeffer begins the chapter on life in community by noting the episode in the Luke's Gospel when the disciples argued about which one of them was the greatest: "No sooner are people together than they begin to observe, judge, and classify each other. . . . [F]rom the first moment two people meet, one begins looking for a competitive position to assume and hold against the other."[2]

In other words, we judge, compare, and condemn.

We can confirm Bonhoeffer's claim simply by observing our own tendencies when meeting others. When we walk into a room of people we don't know, we begin to classify, judge, and make distinctions to "size people up." *Where do I stack up in relationship to these people?* we wonder. We consider the style of their clothes, the shine on their shoes, the provenance of their accent, the make of the car they arrived in. We observe hairstyle and skin complexion and subtle mannerisms. Then our mind employs an unconscious algorithm to tabulate all these data points and dispenses a judgment about which one among us is the greatest. Unlike the disciples, we don't even argue—we can just tell.

Jesus directed much of his ministry at countering this human tendency to pigeonhole others. He refused to condemn a woman caught in adultery and instead invited her accusers to consider their own failings. He refused to impute guilt to a man who was born blind, when others asked whose sins had caused his blindness. He let a woman with a sketchy reputation bathe his feet in ointment at a dinner party and then called out one of the Pharisees at the dinner for his judgmental thoughts. Again and again, Jesus—through his words and deeds—erased the dividing lines of judgment set up by religion and culture and welcomed the judged into fellowship with himself and, through himself, with God.

Even as Jesus gasped for his final breaths, arms and legs nailed to wooden beams, he looked on those who denied him and pierced him and mocked him, and he pleaded with his Abba to forgive them because they did not know what they were doing (see Luke 23:34).

In *Soul Feast*, Marjorie Thompson helpfully lists ways God speaks to us. She reminds us that God can speak to us not only through scripture but also through nature, our own intuitions, the circumstances of our lives, and, of course, other people—*other people.*[3] Each person we encounter is a word from the Lord, a parable of lost-ness and loveliness, a revelation of divine love and mercy and acceptance. But our habits of judgment pull the blinds down on our windows of perception. When we have tidily defined someone by how they walk, act, and speak or by what they eat, listen to, and read, then we have prevented ourselves from seeing them as a revelation of divine love.

Not only do we judge others, we constantly *judge ourselves.*

A couple of paragraphs are insufficient to detail all the ways we weigh ourselves in the balance and more often than not find ourselves wanting. Much of our judgment of others is parasitic on our own self-condemnation that fuels habits of comparison. Social media has exacerbated this tendency by creating a universe in which we encounter the curated and airbrushed lives of our "friends" and wonder what we are doing so wrong that our bodies aren't as sleek, our families as smiley, or our vacations as idyllic. The subtle cry of so many is, *What's wrong with me?*

I witness firsthand self-judgment in relationship to prayer in the lives of my students. I require students in my introduction to spiritual formation course to write weekly journal reflections on their experiences practicing the assigned spiritual disciplines, like praying with scripture, listening to God in silence, and keeping sabbath. I warn them at the beginning of the semester that they will be prone to grading themselves—and *I* don't even grade their journals. I tell them simply to notice their experience and describe it as objectively as they can. Invariably they will write that they "failed" *lectio divina* because they couldn't keep the four steps straight; that they "just can't do" silence because their minds are too busy; that they "were horrible" at keeping sabbath because they felt guilty for not working on a school assignment; that they, in the end, just couldn't "succeed" at prayer. And when I read these journals, I wonder how I taught so poorly that I gave the impression there is any such thing as success in prayer and being good at living a life with God. On the rare occasions when a student declares themselves adept at all things spiritual, I wonder what that could possibly mean. When it comes to life with God, we are always only beginners.

Then I remember their self-judgment has little to do with what I said or didn't say. They are only doing what they were trained to do from the time they could be praised for a beautiful smile or blamed for dropping a spoon laden with strained peas, rewarded for their achievements or condemned for their screw-ups: expressing the internalized judgment of others.

A great gift that comes from approaching life, prayer, and God with a contemplative stance is the ability to lay down these habits of mind, or at least recognize their place within the broader horizon of that gentle, divine embrace that enfolds us every second of our lives.

Finally, of course, we *judge our circumstances.*

We live as if every experience invites us to offer a review as we would for a book we purchased on Amazon or a cottage we rented through Airbnb. The comfort of the chair I'm sitting in: 2.2 stars. The yumminess of this dinner: 3.3 stars. The sunset over the hills: 4.3 (so I photograph it). My arthritis today: 1.1. Accept or reject, pull toward or push away, cling to or toss out—these represent the ways we treat each moment of our lives.

That's why we usually consider another situation preferable to the current one. While stuck in a meeting or a traffic jam, negotiating a conflict between siblings, or scrubbing pans after supper, the morning—warm mug in hand, newspaper on a lap, mockingbird imitating Ella Fitzgerald outside the window—seems infinitely preferable to what we're doing now. It's easy for me to say my children are like Goldilocks, but who *isn't?*

If God makes Godself known to us through the people we encounter, God also allows the circumstances of our lives to become sacraments of Divine Presence, conduits of mercy and grace. This is an insight Frederick Buechner has displayed throughout his writings—especially his memoirs—whether remembering his father's suicide, writing about his vocational discernment, exploring how he grappled with his daughter's eating disorder, or noting the mundane routines of life: "Taking your children to school and kissing your wife good-bye. Eating lunch with a friend. Trying to do a decent day's work. Hearing the rain patter against the window. There is no event so commonplace but that God is present within it, always hiddenly, always leaving you room to recognize him or not to recognize him."[4] The only recipe I know for recognizing this hidden Presence is to pay attention, as I suggested in chapter 3, but I'm certain that our habit of judging our circumstances and giving a thumbs-up or thumbs-down to everything we do and everything that is done to us is a foolproof recipe for missing God in the moment.

> **CONSIDER THIS:**
> Which of these kinds of judgment are you most prone to? What other ways do we judge?

Of course, approaching life with a posture of nonjudgment *doesn't* mean accepting evil when we see it. Injustices of all kinds need to be called out: systemic racism, economic inequity, environmental degradation, and others. But noticing, naming, and resisting injustice is not the same as living with habits of mind that judge *every* circumstance. In fact, only when we let go of our inveterate mental habits of judgment do our minds become free and clear enough to see the world as it really is—a requirement for naming and dismantling injustice.

Life is more complicated than *this is good* and *this is bad*. And if God is present—even hiddenly as Buechner suggests—that presence is hovering just beneath the shallow surface of our lives, the surface we so often fixate on and judge.

Nonjudgment as a Gift

Last spring I planted a garden with the help of my fifteen-year-old son. Early in the 2020 pandemic we were trying, like so many others, to make fertile use of the extra time that working and schooling from home had tossed our way. We cleared, dug, and planted for several weekends. A local nursery delivered seedlings: watermelon and cantaloupe, bell peppers and hot peppers, cabbage and cauliflower, and several varieties of tomatoes. We took a "done is better than perfect" approach, knowing our garden would not win any green-thumb awards or garner a featured spot in the local weekly. We enjoyed most of the work. I especially cherished those silent, companionable hours with my son, listening together to the jazz he is coming to love, our hands working the dirt in tandem.

We only faced one true obstacle: Canada thistle—an invasive, tenacious, and prolific weed.

When God looked at all God had made and declared it good, surely God had overlooked Canada thistle. Much of our gardening time, our biweekly excursions into the side-yard to tend our little plot, involved digging up and tossing out these demonic plants.

So, in the same spring, as I'm praying my way through Matthew's Gospel, I read Jesus' parable of the weeds among the wheat with incredulity (see Matthew 13:24-30). The story's opening makes sense initially: "The kingdom of heaven," Jesus says, "may be compared to someone who sowed good seed in his field; but while everybody was asleep, an enemy came and sowed weeds among the wheat" (vv. 24-25). So far I'm tracking; in fact, I'm nodding vigorously, thinking, *Of course an enemy sowed the weeds!*

They are evil! And I'm picturing the tall, thick-stalked, spiky-leaved invaders from north of the border, the Canadian agricultural equivalent to Russian election meddling—a direct assault on our food supply from an enemy adversary. But the parable turns surreal when the owner of the field tells the servants *not* to gather the weeds. *How could he allow the bad to grow with the good? How could he allow the weeds to crowd the wheat and steal its nutrients?* But the owner has reasons: Pulling up the weeds might uproot the wheat as well. So he instructs the servants to let the good and bad thrive side by side until harvest time, when the wheat will be collected first and the weeds burned. *At least the weeds will get what they deserve in the end.*

As Jesus explains later in the chapter, this parable has an eschatological function—it points to God's intention in the end to "collect out of his kingdom all causes of sin and all evildoers" and shovel them into a fiery furnace "where there will be weeping and gnashing of teeth" (vv. 41-42). When the story of God's creation comes to an end, there will, according to Jesus' interpretation of his own parable, be a cleansing, a refining, so that only righteousness will remain.

Some of us flinch at the idea of God's separating the wheat from the weeds when they represent people. *Really,* we wonder, *will God consign the "weeds" to a consuming fire?* We find it even more repellent than I find the notion that plants like Canada thistle might be allowed to linger and live. Enough passages throughout the New Testament suggest the possibility that in the end God will reconcile all things to the ways of love and shalom that I don't fret too much about this hyperbolic language, aimed at assuring frightened first-century disciples that God's kingdom will ultimately prevail.

But there's a richer meaning for us today as we read this parable from which we might gain a sense of freedom: If any separating needs to be done, any thinning of the metaphorical weeds from the field of humanity, *it's not our job to do it.* Only a God who would hang on a cross and plead for his murderers' forgiveness has the character to pass judgment. Only an all-knowing and profoundly merciful God has the patience and insight to distinguish between weeds and wheat. Only a God whose nature is love can be trusted with such delicate work.

Only the One who created has the right to judge the creation. Not us.

We have been given our lives by God. We don't need to judge them.

We have been offered these moments as jewels from God's hand. We don't need to reject them.

We have been tossed into a world populated with "weeds" and "wheat," all of which bear Christ's image and neither of which can we tell apart with certainty. There is weed and wheat in each one of us. Under these conditions, we have no business playing the jury.

> **CONSIDER THIS:** What do you think about the idea that God is the only one gracious, loving, and wise enough to judge? Do you find that liberating? Why or why not?

Can you feel the liberating potential of this insight? The burden of judging others and ourselves and the circumstances of our lives makes us like a man trying to carry three heavy bags of groceries to the house from the car. He's burdened, bent over, off balance, fighting gravity to keep each bag off the ground. Then a stranger approaches—tall, strong, gracious—and says, "Let me help you with those," and takes the bags out of the man's hands. Relieved of his burden, he can stand straight and walk again with purpose and meaning. We've each been there, the burdened pack-mule carrying awkward packages, so we know how delightful such liberation feels.

God says to us:

Here, let me take those bags, the responsibility you've felt for so long to judge. You don't need them anymore. If anyone should have them, it's me. Be free to live in this world, to enjoy it. Be curious about your world, pay close attention to it, thrive in it, without the burden of needing to judge it, to label every experience, to cleanse it from what you deem unseemly. Enjoy your friends and family with such freedom, your coworkers and neighbors with such grace. Relish my creation without grading it. Find me in each moment without needing to give the moment a review. Delight in the *you* I've created you to be without rejecting the less-than-pristine parts of who you are.

Silence—Laboratory for Nonjudgment

From the earliest days of Christianity, followers of Jesus knew that silence is necessary for fostering an attitude of nonjudgment. Early Christian monks—known as the desert fathers and mothers because they moved into the deserts of Egypt, Syria, and Palestine in the third and fourth centuries to practice lives of full surrender to God—looked to Jesus as the model of contemplative silence: He woke early and found places of solitude to pray away from the clamoring throngs.

And wasn't he the one who admonished his followers not to judge?

Since these monks recognized that judgment begins in thoughts before it ever finds expression in words or actions, they cultivated practices of awareness that helped them see and observe their thoughts without judging them so they could get some distance from them and prevent these thoughts from controlling them. The monks called this *practicing vigilance*. The idea is to notice thoughts as they arise—without clinging to them or engaging them—before they become rooted in the heart.

Many popular approaches to silence today resemble the practice of these early monastics, even secular approaches. Mindful silence for instance often looks like what Christian monks have been doing for centuries: sitting in silence, observing thoughts without judgment, neither clinging to nor rejecting them but simply letting them arise and float away like clouds on the wind, without getting lost in them.

In the book *What We Need Is Here*, I outlined a practice of silence that involves focusing on a prayer word or phrase that's repeated in the mind to free us from the thoughts we get lost in.[5] This way of practicing silence is rooted in the Eastern Orthodox tradition of saying the Jesus Prayer ("Lord Jesus Christ, Son of God, have mercy on me, a sinner") and found its most eloquent twentieth-century advocate in John Main, a Benedictine monk. It finds what I believe to be its most penetrating contemporary expression in the work of theologian and Augustinian monk Martin Laird.[6] Laird summarizes the practice beautifully when he writes, "And so when we sit, we give our full attention wholly to the gentle repetition of the prayer word. We will find that our attention is forever being stolen. As soon as we become aware that our attention has been stolen by some thought, we gently bring ourselves back to the prayer word."[7] Imagine a camera with a zoom lens. This practice zooms in—it focuses—on a word or phrase (or an object or image) to help achieve freedom from the whirlwind of thoughts.

TRY THIS: Set a timer for three minutes and sit in silence, repeating in your mind the name "Jesus," giving it your full attention. When your mind wanders, simply return to the repetition of the word.

Another approach to silence is zooming out instead of in. I have found this approach helpful in becoming more aware of the content of our thoughts. It helps us to see how much of our thinking involves judgment—deciding something is good and clinging to it or declaring something bad and rejecting it. Rather than focusing our attention, this method invites us to widen the scope of our awareness so that we watch our thoughts as they float by. The fact is, we have thoughts we can't control, but we don't have to *think* them—we don't have to take that original thought and whip it into a froth, turn it into a story that then stirs up our emotions until we are completely lost in it. This prayerful awareness helps us become just that—aware of these thoughts and the power they have over us, without necessarily giiving in to them. James Finley, a contemporary teacher of Christian meditation, expresses this approach to thoughts succinctly: "With respect to the mind, the guideline is to be present, open, and awake, neither clinging to nor rejecting anything."[8]

> **TRY THIS:** Set a timer for three minutes and sit in silence, not focusing on any one thing but watching your thoughts as they arise. If you find yourself lost in a thought, simply release it and return to a posture of observing.

Watch the thoughts—notice them—but don't engage. Let them pass, and they will.

At first we might be amazed—or, more likely, appalled—at the angry, judgmental, gossipy nature of our thoughts: *Is this really in me?* And then we will be tempted to judge ourselves for our judgmental thoughts. But *that* thought is just one more link in the chain of thoughts, so notice it with whatever self-compassion you can muster, and let it dissolve, too.

And remember what the desert monks learned from Jesus: In this silent watching, God is present, caring for us, loving us, reminding us who we really are—people who don't get it right all the time; people who are loved and forgiven; people on a journey of getting better; people who are infinitely welcomed into the infinitely loving embrace of the One who created us.

Our own learning not to judge ourselves or our thoughts arises out of God's own gracious acceptance of ourselves just as we are—and of our neighbors just as they are.

Taking a Walk

Yesterday my eleven-year-old daughter, Mary Clare, joined me on a walk. This time, *I* was Goldilocks. Nothing on the walk went right. We reached the elementary school just as the buses were spilling out onto the road, zooming past way too close to us (because of the pandemic, my daughter was attending school virtually). "I couldn't have picked a worse time to take a walk," I said to the police officer who was directing traffic. Then, trying to maneuver around a construction crew ripping up the road to install water pipes, we almost got hit by a swiveling backhoe—I had to push Mary Clare out of the way. In the process, I slipped on gravel and hurt my hip. "This is a horrible walk!" I shouted.

"Now, Dad," Mary Clare said, "you should say: 'I'm taking a walk with my daughter, enjoying being outdoors, and encountering a few obstacles. This is not what I would prefer, but I won't let this keep me from walking outdoors' "—that latter bit was inspired by my mumbling something about never taking a walk again.

So today I try again. I want to practice a posture of nonjudgment. I want to learn to welcome what comes my way. I put on a coat, scarf, and my earflap-equipped cap. I plant earbuds in my ears, stash my phone in a coat pocket, and head out.

As I leave, my young adviser yells to me, "Dad! What are you doing? Look at the time—the school buses will be out again."

Equanimity prevails. "What will be, will be," I say.

And I discover that we *can* adopt this posture of openness and non-judgment, if we remain aware. The wind chapping my face doesn't send me back home; I cover my cheeks with my scarf and notice the change from cold to warm, each feeling pleasant in its own way. As the buses whiz past me, instead of cursing them, I notice them—how they are packed with kids eager to get home and chill, and I can remember my own daily relief at the end of the school day when I was a child. Halfway through the walk, my back and head are sweating. I loosen my scarf and carry my cap, marveling at the way our bodies regulate temperature. A song on the playlist I'm listening to begins. It's one I don't particularly like and usually skip, but not this time. I listen to the words in a way I never have before. "You don't have to *like* it to appreciate it," I imagine my daughter saying to me.

Goldilocks didn't have to *like* the temperature of the porridge to be nourished by it, after all.

And I'm reminded of Merton again. "For it is God's love that warms me in the sun and God's love that sends the cold rain. It is God's love that feeds me in the bread I eat and God that feeds me also by hunger and fasting."[9]

God is feeding me in the wind chapping my cheeks, the tunes pleasing my ear, the thoughts floating through my mind. God is feeding me through the pumping of my legs up a hill, the puffing of my lungs for breath, the sweating of my brow under a wool cap. And I'm learning that, if God is in it—whatever *it* happens to be at the moment—and I am open to it, then my judgments about it begin to fade away.

Spiritual Exercises

Sacred Reading

Matthew 13:24-30; Luke 9:46-47; 1 Corinthians 12:12-31
(See directions for sacred reading on page 155.)

Practicing Awareness

Take fifteen minutes and, in a spirit of prayer and with an attitude of openness to God, use these questions to look over yesterday or last week:

- When did I notice my tendency to judge during this time?

- When did I judge others, myself, or my circumstances?
- How did that judgment contribute to or diminish my sense of well-being or my openness to God?
- Were there times when I was able to accept my circumstances without judgment? How did this affect my sense of God's presence?
- What am I learning about myself and my relationship to God as I reflect on my habits of judgment?

Close with prayer, giving thanks for what God has shown you and asking God to help you be more aware of and responsive to God's loving agency in your life.

Prompts for Journaling

Write a letter to God about your desire to approach life nonjudgmentally—or your confusion about what that means. Tell God about your habits of judging yourself, others, and your circumstances. In your own words, write about how you would like to be free from judgment, to cherish others and yourself with something more like God's own gracious acceptance. Write anything else that seems significant to you right now.

Now, write a letter to yourself *from* God. How do you imagine God would respond to the letter you wrote to God?

8

Raising Our Anchors

Freedom

The freedom of love and realization of union leads to active participation *in* God. Here one not only recognizes one's own beauty and precious nature, but also shares God's love and compassion for others in real, practical service in the world.

—GERALD MAY, *THE DARK NIGHT OF THE SOUL*

When I was in seventh grade, my older brother and I spent a weekend with our grandparents. Grammy and Pap were ideal grandparents, always game to do more with grandchildren than play Parcheesi and shuffleboard, though we did slide our fair share of pucks down concrete slabs.

During our visit, they took us to a state park for a picnic. After we ate, Pap opted for a quiet afternoon of fishing while Grammy elected something more adventurous: to row with us out to an island in the middle of a lake on a blustery spring day. I think she even volunteered to row, but we claimed that privilege. The voyage to the island was slow going; a fierce headwind impeded our progress. My brother struggled to sustain forward momentum, while Grammy and I relaxed like vacationers in a Venetian gondola.

When we finally arrived, we surveyed the small island like Charles Darwin in the Galapagos.

I seized the oars on the return trip, expecting to journey with ease, impelled as we were by the wind at our backs. I rowed with vigor to get us started, hoping soon to let the breeze take over, but after a few minutes we seemed no further from the island and no closer to the shore. Our progress halted completely thirty yards out. We veered some to the left and then some to the right, but we never went forward despite my vigorous rowing. My arms began to ache.

That's when I heard the giggling and turned around to see Grammy and my brother buckled over with laughter.

"Why are you laughing?" I asked.

My brother grabbed a rope and began pulling it slowly out of the water, allowing its wet lengths to curl in the bottom of the boat until an anchor appeared over the side, dripping. He hoisted the anchor into the boat, revealing the practical joke they had played on me. With an anchor caught on jagged rocks at the bottom of the lake, I was helpless to coerce the boat forward. Once free of the anchor's weight, we glided effortlessly across the waves.

From the early days of the church, Christians have used the image of a sailboat to describe a contemplative life with God. Our practices of prayer are the sails we open to catch the wind of God's Spirit moving us in the direction of God's leading. With our sails open—with our lives open and available to God—we can respond to God.

Unless an anchor is dropped.

Imagine a heavy metal anchor sunk into the bottom of a lake, its barbs snagged on rocks and debris. Under those conditions, the sailboat of our lives—like the rowboat I was fruitlessly rowing—won't go anywhere. We're stuck.

Most of us know that feeling. We have begun to discern God's intention for our lives. Perhaps we sense a calling to serve others in a way that feels risky—to change jobs, to go back to school, or to end a destructive relationship that's bad for us. Perhaps we detect God inviting us to commit to a cause that will require a sacrifice of time or money. Perhaps we see the growing movements around us for racial equality and economic justice and feel drawn to be a part. In some way, we sense the wind filling our sails.

But something holds us back. Somewhere within us there is a catch, a place of *un*-freedom. A fear prevents us from acting. A destructive habit holds us in a place. An aversion precludes our movement. Or we cling to an image of ourselves or an image of God—and that clinging acts like an anchor caught on submerged rocks.

If we want to live as everyday contemplatives—open, available, and responsive to God—we need to live in freedom. We need to see clearly the anchors that are dropped so God can set us free of them.

Another Name for the Anchor

Ignatius of Loyola, founder of the Jesuits in the sixteenth century, calls those things we cling to inordinately *attachments*, or sometimes *disordered attachments*.[1] According to this Christian tradition (and others as well, especially the Carmelite tradition of Teresa of Avila and John of the Cross) an attachment names anything that we are so stuck to we are prevented from recognizing what is good and necessary and godly. Attachments cloud our perception of the presence and call of God. And you can be attached to almost anything: a

> **CONSIDER THIS:**
> What does the word *attachment* connote for you? How would you describe in your own words what an attachment is?

person, a car, an idea, a style of worship, an experience of God, a certain way of prayer—even an image of God.

Many of us are attached to our plans for our lives. Some of us are attached to our plans for *other* people's lives.

We can also become attached to images of ourselves.

It could be a fruitful (and perhaps painful) spiritual exercise to ask what images of yourself give you a sense of security or identity. What images of yourself do you fear having wrenched from you? What identity-giving image are you grasping onto for dear life, like a sailor tossed into the sea and clinging to a life-preserver? Here are some possible contenders: the competent one; the wise one; the martyr, hero, or messiah. When we become attached to images of ourselves, we pull other things and people into our orbit to shore up our sense of self. We use our jobs, positions in society, and relationships to secure an identity we fear living without.

It's not always a lofty image. We usually associate clinging to a false image of ourselves with pride, but notice how Thomas Merton defines *pride*: "Pride is a stubborn insistence on being what we are not and never were intended to be. Pride is a deep, insatiable need for unreality, an exorbitant demand that others believe the lie we have made ourselves believe about ourselves."[2]

That false, prideful image can just as easily be of one who is helpless or incapable—a failure who is worthless, unloved, and unlovable. These ways of imagining ourselves often derive from outside influences—our families of origin, early experiences in school, wider cultural norms. As painful as these inherited or internalized images can be, they can still give us a sense of identity. Why would we cling to them? Maybe because an image we are familiar with, however much suffering it causes us, feels more secure than having no self-image at all.

Consider Merton's point: When we are attached to an image of ourselves, we are *clinging to unreality*. Many of us nurture this unreality by engaging in what theologian Rowan Williams calls "self-dramatizing and fantasy."[3] The false identity we have created for ourselves—or others have created for us—becomes a fantastical reality we inhabit, whether that "reality" brings us pleasure or pain. I suspect many of us cling to some combination of false images of uber-competence and incompetence at the same time, images that shape our lives for the worse.

> **TRY THIS:** Write for ten minutes in a journal about images of yourself that you have held over the years. What did it feel like when these were challenged? Which ones do you still hold on to?

We can be attached to many things—agendas for our lives and the lives of others, images of ourselves, physical possessions, or positions of privilege. You name it; you can become attached to it. The lesson is that we can't truly serve God and others if we are held back, anchored in place by disordered attachments.

We can't be available and responsive to God.

We need to find freedom.

The Opposite of Being Attached

Imagine this not unlikely scenario: I'm in my office, hungry at mid-morning, sitting on a small sofa grading papers, when I get a mental image that I naturally take to be the inspiration of the Holy Spirit: a plate of fried crab wontons from my favorite Chinese restaurant. *Could this be a sign from God that our family should have Chinese food for dinner?* I wonder. I spend the greater part of the day failing to accomplish my work tasks because I'm too distracted by a growling stomach and the blissful anticipation of dinner.

When I arrive home, I announce to my children, "Good news! We're going out to dinner!" Before I can tell them my plan, they begin excitedly discussing among themselves where we should go. One runs into the other room and tells his mother, "Dad says we're going out to dinner—and we know where we want to go!"

Before I know it, I'm in the passenger seat of a van with three giddy children in the back, on my way to a second-rate chain restaurant that, like every other chain, has a dining room decorated with local high school paraphernalia, posters of Elvis and Marilyn Monroe, and crookedly hung musical instruments. The top-selling appetizer will not be fried crab wontons but some variety of a deep-fried onion with a side of spicy ranch dressing. A tin of peanuts sits on the table, and peanut shells are scattered on the floor.

How will I respond to this dashed hope? Am I ruined for the rest of the night—grouchy, despondent, unable to even pretend to enjoy my overcooked Southwest chipotle burger, bitter at having my chief desire of the day—for Chinese food—left unfulfilled? Will I pout through dinner and act petulant the rest of the night?

If I'm too attached to my food, the answer will be yes.

But what if—hypothetically speaking—I possess the quality of spirit that Ignatius of Loyola says is the opposite of having disordered attachments, a quality he dubbed (rather unfortunately) *indifference*?

When we hear the word *indifference*, we typically think it means "not caring." But for Ignatius, indifference indicates inner freedom.[4] It means the anchors in the soul have been hoisted and stowed. In the case of my dinner, being indifferent wouldn't have required my not wanting or even not preferring Chinese. It would have meant, rather, that I was free enough from my desire for Chinese food—from getting *my* way—that I could good-naturedly roll with a situation I didn't ask for.

This scenario is an inconsequential example. But when the question becomes being responsive to God in prayer and in life, the stakes are higher.

Jesus told a story of a man who'd been robbed, beaten, stripped, and thrown to the side of the road (see Luke 10:25-37). Two people, both religious leaders, saw the suffering man and crossed the street to avoid him. Why they did this is unclear. Perhaps they feared contact with the man would render them religiously unclean. Maybe they worried that the robbers were lurking nearby, and the man was bait for their next victim. Maybe they were in a hurry—they had a plan for their day—and couldn't be sidetracked. It's certainly plausible to say that a posture of un-freedom—disordered attachments—kept them from responding to this man in love. Their anchors were dropped.

> **CONSIDER THIS:**
> How do you react to the word *indifference*? After reading about what it means, how would you put it in your own words?

But another man came by as well, a foreigner who many would presume harbored an animosity toward the wounded man. Without hesitation he took a detour, suspending his own plans so he could care for the injured man. His time, energy, and resources were freely available to be used for the victim's healing. He possessed inner freedom. He had no anchor.

James Martin, a Jesuit scholar and writer, offers another example from his own life of inner freedom—indifference. Martin said in an interview with Krista Tippett that when he was a young priest in training, he met with his superior for a conversation about where his place of ministry should be. He told his superior, "Well, you know what? The last thing I want to do is work in a hospital. I don't think I could stand that, the smells and the sights and the sounds."

His superior said, "Well, good. Then you'll be working in a hospital."

Martin understood the decision of his superior, who knew that Martin needed to be free to serve wherever God might want him. "Imagine a priest who was so unfree that he couldn't set foot in a hospital," he said.

Martin summarized the perspective of Ignatius of Loyola: "Ignatius wanted us to be free of anything that kept us from following God. He called them disordered attachments. And the idea is that if anything keeps you from being more open to God's will in your life, get rid of it."[5]

> **CONSIDER THIS:** Think of a time in your life when you needed inner freedom in order to do something you sensed God was asking you to do. What held you back?

Ignatius didn't invent the notion of inner freedom—he'd read his Bible.

Paul affirms the importance of inner freedom—of releasing attachments—to respond to God, to serve God in all circumstances. Paul writes, "I know what it is to have little, and I know what it is to have plenty. In any and all circumstances I have learned the secret of being well-fed and of going hungry, of having plenty and of being in need. I can do all things through [Christ] who strengthens me" (Phil. 4:12-13). Paul's inner freedom allows him to serve God in all circumstances. He doesn't have to deny that being well fed is better than going hungry—of course it is—to claim that an attachment to food shouldn't keep him from responding freely to God in love and relying on the grace of Christ in every situation.

Apparently, I could learn something from Paul.

Following Paul, maybe I could say, "I have learned the secret of enjoying fried wontons—and of bland chain-food fare. I can do all things through Christ."

Moving Toward Freedom

So what do we do?

How do we loosen our grip so we're not trying to control life based on our own anxious attachments and agendas? How do we recognize them and begin to let them go—or let God pry them out of our grasp? We cannot will ourselves into a posture of freedom. Only God's Spirit working in us can free us from our attachments and bring us the joy that comes with freedom. This is God's work.

God is doing that work. Christians in Wesleyan traditions name that the work of *prevenient grace*—God's action to liberate us to respond in freedom to God. Then we can cooperate with God, further opening ourselves to God's grace so that the liberation goes as deep as possible. We continue to recognize places of attachments—we discover anchors that are holding us back—and then we open those areas of our lives to God's grace.

The process continues, I imagine, our whole lives.

If we can't achieve freedom on our own, we *can* become increasingly aware of places we are *not* free and offer those places to God. A few steps can help us increase that awareness.

The first step to recognizing and releasing our attachments is to *notice* them. We need to become skilled at noticing when attachments are holding us back. And that means paying attention. (I told you in the introduction that these different aspects of an open, available posture are interrelated.) In particular, we can practice noticing our feelings and our thoughts.

We can pay attention to our *feelings*—anxieties and fears or the kind of sadness that creeps around the edges of our lives. In what situations do we feel anxious, fearful, sad, disturbed, or frustrated? At this stage, we are just noticing, not trying to *do* anything. There are many reasons we register these feelings. It's possible that they could indicate that an attachment is being threatened or that an image of ourselves is being undermined.

A nightly practice of an Examen can help us to become more attuned to these emotions.

We should also notice our *thoughts*. Do we perseverate by fixating on something in our minds? Do we fantasize or engage in self-dramatization? These kinds of obsessive thoughts can point to places of un-freedom. At one point in my teaching career, I was upset that I was being denied what I considered a reasonable request to come up for tenure a couple of years early. When I kept throwing mental temper tantrums months after the situation passed, I had to ask myself if there was an image of myself at risk—perhaps the overachiever or the one who deserves special attention and accolades. When we're mentally acting like frustrated toddlers, that's a pretty good indication of an attachment.

> **TRY THIS:** Take some time to examine your habitual thoughts and feelings over the last week. Do any indicate a fear of losing something you are attached to?

When we notice these things—these anxious feelings, the sense of threat, the self-dramatization—we wonder if there might be a hidden attachment at play. A light bulb flashes on. We begin to pay closer attention.

After we notice, we start to *probe*. We hit the pause button, step back, and look more deeply. We ask ourselves: *Why am I feeling this way? Why am I acting this way? What am I afraid of? Is there something I want—a way I want to be, perhaps, or a way I want someone else to be—that I'm afraid won't work out?* We pull out the flashlight and peer into the corners of our soul.

Maybe we want to probe or process this with a trusted friend, someone we can talk things out with. Maybe we want to do it on our own, perhaps writing in a journal. I have often written myself into a more penetrating awareness. Either way, it takes time. And either way, when we are in prayer, we ask God for insight: *God, help me see beneath this to what's really going on, and bring me to inner freedom.*

Next, we might find it helpful to *name* what we are discovering. After our awareness deepens through our own prayerful investigations, it can be helpful to put words to what we are finding. What conclusion has our probing brought us to? We can write it down, being as specific as possible. We might write something like, "I realize now that I'm afraid my image of myself as the most competent one might prove to be false," or "I'm afraid people won't like me," or "I'm discovering hidden racial prejudice I didn't know was there." When we can name something in this way, whatever it is will have much less power over us. The anchor has lost some of its weight when we know it's there.

After we name what we are discovering, we might want to *speak* it to another. The sayings of the early Christian monks living in the desert are replete with stories about young monks who keep secrets from their elders (one monk had a habit of stealing bread). Only when the younger monk can speak aloud the secret attachment ("I've been stealing bread!"), does inner freedom come. In one story, the attachment is shown as a demon flying from a young monk's heart.[6]

I don't expect to see flying demons when I confess my attachments. Nor do I anticipate freedom to come instantly. But I do know there is freedom in speaking. Imagine how powerful it could be, for instance, for a man to say to his wife and children: "I've been noticing how angry and frustrated I've been in the evening, and it's been really bothering me. I realize that I have an image of how the evening should go: I remember seeing my dad quietly reading the paper every night, and I somehow imagine that's the way it should be for me too. But that makes me angry with you all—and the dog—when you make noise or want my attention. I think God is showing me that availability to my family in the evening is more important than my peace and quiet, than my image of how an evening should go. So that's what I see. I'm not sure what to do, because I need quiet like I need food, but that shouldn't ruin our evenings."

No demon will fly from the father's breast. But in speaking aloud what God is showing him, he will find more freedom to be open to God, who is present to him even in the screaming of a child and the barking of a dog.

Finally, we must *act*—we act in a way that is consistent with how we want to be and with what we know is right, even if our feelings have yet to catch up. We walk into the hospital even if the sights, sounds, and smells repel us, if that's where God is leading. We cross the street and offer aid to a wounded man, even if our fear warns us to stay on our side. We exercise what little freedom the Spirit has wrought in us, knowing such action paves the pathway to greater awareness and even deeper liberation.

What's Possible When We Are Free

Thomas Kelly, a Quaker mystic and author of the spiritual classic *A Testament of Devotion*, uses a Quaker term to describe what's possible when we approach God and life with a posture of inner freedom: We are able to discern a *concern*.[7] A concern describes a special burden one feels for some aspect of a situation in the world. God has a cosmic concern for the whole world, but we don't have the time, energy, or resources to direct our attention to every good cause. We are not God. What we *do* have is the capacity to notice how God is moving us to respond to a circumstance and—if we have a degree of inner freedom—act.

In the summer of 1938, Kelly traveled to Germany to give a prestigious lecture at the yearly meeting of Friends. He spent two months there and witnessed firsthand the persecution of Jews. He addressed German Quakers who were wondering how to resist the Nazi government and love well their Jewish neighbors amid fear of reprisals. He reminded them of a central practice of discerning a concern. "We cannot carry *all* burdens," he told them, "nor die on *all* crosses, desperately as they need to be borne and suffered."[8] But we can discern, he told them, how God's cosmic concern for the world can become particularized in our own lives and communities. He writes elsewhere that God "speaks within you and me, to our truest selves, in our truest moments, and disquiets us with the world's needs. By inner persuasions [God] draws us to a few very definite tasks, *our* tasks, God's burdened heart particularizing [God's] burdens in us."[9] God's universal compassion can become concrete in our lives.

After the school shooting in Parkland, Florida, my wife organized our local congregation to write letters to state and national representatives advocating for stricter gun laws. She'd already been writing these letters herself but sensed an inner persuasion to widen the effort. She spoke with our pastor, designed flyers for the bulletin, and made announcements in worship—and three weeks after the shooting, our congregation placed several dozen letters on the altar and prayed over them. In her actions I witnessed a posture of freedom: open listening to God combined with the willingness to act, even if everyone in the congregation didn't agree with her.

> **CONSIDER THIS:** What concern is God drawing you toward right now? How are you recognizing it? What would it take to say yes to God?

More recently, our family has sensed that God is burdening our hearts to address issues of racism in our own lives, the institutions in which we work, and our community. As it did for so many white people who didn't believe we were complicit in racism, the murder of George Floyd in May of 2020 became a harsh alarm bell, awakening us from our complacent sense of moral righteousness. We knew that we had to learn more, become more aware of how racism was infecting our own lives, begin to speak with our children, and act in the communities of which we were a part. What attachment could be worse than the racism and ideology of white supremacy that holds so many people in its vise-grip?

So we listened to podcasts with our children. We took them to protests. We had frank conversations with them about race. Since this was during the pandemic in 2020, we hosted an online book study with white friends from across the country on anti-racist parenting. I became more vocal in the seminary where I work about the need to address our own institutional racism, and Ginger began to work to shape conversations around racism at the majority-white congregation where she works—with not a little pushback.

We are not heroes. This is just the beginning of what should be done. We are only beginning to explore what freedom means when it comes to questions of racism, and we have much more learning to do about how the anchors of racism are still lodged in the depths of our spirits. But it *is* an example of how, when we are open to God—listening and willing—God speaks "within you and me," as Kelly put it, "to our truest selves, in our truest moments, and disquiets us with the world's needs." It is an example of God's "burdened heart particularizing [God's] burdens in us."

Free Indeed

It's been many years since my shoulders ached on that rowboat with my brother and grandmother, as I fruitlessly slapped oars into the waves over and over again, getting nowhere. But I think about that day often as I try to imagine life with God. In how much of my life am I dragging oars through the water but getting nowhere because an anchor has been dropped?

Fortunately, being servants to our attachments doesn't have to be the full story. I've seen so many people open their lives to God, taste a hint of freedom, and then open even more as God's Spirit has transformed their stuck lives into nimble sailboats dancing on the waves, responding to the winds of grace, splashing forward in hope, pressed onward in freedom by love.

As the apostle Paul wrote, "For freedom Christ has set us free" (Gal. 5:1). And as Jesus said, "So if the Son makes you free, you will be free indeed" (John 8:36).

Spiritual Exercises

Sacred Reading

Romans 7:15–8:4; Philippians 4:8-14; Luke 4:16-21
(See directions for sacred reading on page 155.)

Practicing Awareness

Take some time and reflect on the last six to eight months of your life. Where in your life, work, or relationships do you see evidence that an attachment is at play? What makes you think so? What have been the consequences? How has it gotten in the way of your openness, availability, and responsiveness to God?

Follow the five steps outlined in the chapter to get a better sense of how attachments might be keeping you stuck:

- *Notice:* Feelings and Thoughts
- *Probe:* Ask for Insight

What is going on beneath those feelings or thoughts? Is there something you are afraid of losing? Is there something you don't want to change? Is there something you are afraid will change in the wrong way?

- *Name:* In one, clear, succinct sentence, name the attachment you've been exploring here.
- *Speak:* To whom could you talk about this?
- *Act:* How do you want to act now that you have a deeper awareness of this attachment?

Close with prayer, giving thanks for what God has shown you and asking God to help you to be more aware of and responsive to God's loving agency in your life.

Prompts for Journaling

Write a letter to God about your struggles with attachments. Share where you sense un-freedom in your life. Ask God to continue to give you insight and clarity into your struggle. Maybe you have some resistance to letting go of your attachments; write to God about this as well. Ask God in your own words to help you come to greater inner freedom. Or write to God about a concern for some situation you are sensing in your life, perhaps something God is calling you to. Ask God to give you the courage to say yes.

Now, write a letter to yourself *from* God. How do you imagine God would respond to the letter you wrote to God?

CONCLUSION

The wholly obedient life is mastered and unified and sim-
plified and gathered up into the love of God and it lives
and walks among [people] in the perpetual flame of that
radiant love.

—THOMAS R. KELLY, *A Testament of Devotion*

'm not sitting in my green La-Z-Boy. It's in the basement next to my desk
in my makeshift pandemic office and has been since I started working,
writing, and teaching from home almost a year ago. Also, a teenager lives
in the basement, which makes it a less than ideal environment for solitude
and prayer.

The chair I'm currently sitting in is tucked in the corner of our bedroom. It's a wingback with paisley upholstery, nothing close to the style we
would choose. It rests here safely out of view. I needed a reading chair in
my office at the seminary, so I claimed this one from the seminary library
when it was being renovated and they were giving away furniture. I lugged
it home from my office a year ago. It's one of a matching pair. I wonder if
it misses its mate.

Today is February 2. Cold. Our bedroom sits above the garage, making
it the coldest room in the house. One of the many afghans my wife has cro-
cheted in the past few months warms my legs. The dull light of an overcast
morning presses through the window.

Many folks are thinking this morning about a groundhog named Phil in a tricky-to-spell Pennsylvania town eighty miles northeast of where I am. Phil's handlers, outfitted in bow ties and top hats, have already announced that Phil has seen his shadow, which suggests this afghan will get plenty more use before spring.

Fewer people call today by its other name, its name on the Christian calendar: the Feast of the Presentation of Jesus. The second chapter of Luke tells the story of Mary and Joseph dedicating their firstborn son to God at the Temple in Jerusalem (see Luke 2:22-35). At the time, Jesus was just over a month old.

So, while others are pondering a rodent weather forecaster, I'm reading a touching story of two parents taking their newborn on his first trip out of town and meeting an old man named Simeon.

Open-Armed

It's worth attending to the details of Simeon's story because he exemplifies the posture toward life with God I've been describing in this book.

Scripture says the "Holy Spirit rested on him" (Luke 2:25) and that it "had been revealed to him by the Holy Spirit" that he would see the Messiah before he died (Luke 2:26). On the day Mary and Joseph brought Jesus to the Temple, Simeon himself was "guided by the Spirit" to show up as well (Luke 2:27). There, Simeon opened wide his arms and held the baby. He was able to see something about Jesus others couldn't yet see. He praised God, declaring the truth of what he saw about the child and announcing that Jesus would be "a light for revelation to the Gentiles and for glory to [God's] people Israel" (Luke 2:32).

A picture begins to emerge of one living completely open, available, and responsive to God, of a man free from defenses and attachments, sensitive to the Holy Spirit's presence and action in his life. He was a servant of God able to respond in the moment to the shifting wind of God's Spirit. This posture of responsiveness and freedom in God allowed him to see the good news of God's saving grace in an unlikely place: the squirming bundle in his arms.

He was a boat without an anchor, sails raised and open to the Spirit of God.

Simeon was an everyday contemplative.

Simeon has always been an important figure for me. For at least twenty years, I've prayed the Song of Simeon before bed every night, longing to be as open and responsive to God as he. We named our first child after him because we wanted to be open enough to see in him what God sees, to know that this child is a word from God to us, a gift in the world. We wanted to see him as everyday contemplatives might.

> **TRY THIS:** Read the story of Simeon in Luke 2:22-35. Then review the chapters in this book. Which of the seven characteristics of a contemplative posture do you see in Simeon?

There are a lot of feast days on the Christian calendar. Many of them I've never heard of; others I've heard of but don't remember. But there are some I never fail to observe in some small way, because the figures they memorialize are figures that reflect for me the kind of life I long to live: open, available, responsive to God.

On March 17, I think of St. Patrick. How many people possess the freedom in God to take God's news of restoration and forgiveness to the people who had once enslaved them?

On March 25, the Feast of the Annunciation, I meditate on the angel showing up to Mary and delivering unbelievable news. I also meditate on Mary's unconditional yes to God.

On February 14, I observe St. Valentine's Day. Because: chocolate.

And on February 2, I consider an old man who kept an eye out for God's Messiah. Who trusted God's promises. Who watched and waited, sensitive to the presence and movement of God's Spirit in his life. Who was free enough from attachments to respond to the Spirit's gentle nudge to go when God said, "Go." Who was vulnerable enough to say to Mary and Joseph the truth he saw in their child. Who opened his arms and held God's long-awaited gift before he died, then offered his life back to God, saying, "Master, now you are dismissing your servant in peace" (Luke 2:29).

He'd seen God's Messiah and had held the holy child in his arms—what more did he need?

A Bold Suggestion

Is it too bold to suggest that we too could live like St. Patrick, Mary, or Simeon—like so many of the saints who lived each moment of their lives radically open to God, completely available, responsive to the invitations of divine love coursing in and around them? This is what I'm wondering as I sit in a cold bedroom and consider Simeon. Can we approach life, prayer, and God—indeed, each moment given to us—as everyday contemplatives with a posture composed of the following characteristics?

- *Longing*—letting our natural desire for God guide us through life.
- *Attention*—watching for glimpses of grace in every part of our lives.
- *Patience*—growing increasingly okay with not being in control.
- *Playfulness*—relaxing in the presence of a God who makes all things new.
- *Vulnerability*—offering our authentic selves to God and neighbor.
- *Nonjudgment*—receiving with grace the people and circumstances of our lives.
- *Freedom*—responding with yes to the concerns God inspires in us.

There is no gym where we can lift soul-weights that will bring this posture about. There is no strategic seven-point plan that will guarantee a contemplative approach to life analogous to the plans sold by magazines each summer promising a beach body in a few short weeks.

But there is a God who can shape this posture in us, who can take what we show up with and work with that. What we show up with is all God needs—that and our grace-enabled consent, our open-hearted yes.

> **CONSIDER THIS:**
> Review the list of characteristics of a contemplative posture. Which ones feel natural to you? Which ones do you feel less at home with? Why is this so?

One More Letter to God

I'm realizing something here at the end of this short book.

Along the way, in the spiritual exercises at the end of each chapter, I have invited you to write letters to God. This book is not addressed to God like Augustine's *Confessions*, which moves back and forth between something like memoir and something like prayer. It's addressed to you the reader. I have tried to imagine you—the questions you bring, the challenges you face, the hopes you harbor, suspecting they are not so different from my own.

Yet on another level, this book is a kind of prayer because I have no doubt God has been eavesdropping, looking over my shoulder, able to see my own deep longing in what I'm writing to you. Able to spy in these pages a prayer: *Help me, O God, to follow my longing, pay attention, embody patience, enjoy playfulness, embrace vulnerability, practice nonjudgment, and respond in freedom—all so that I can be a word from you that bears your love into the world.*

Maybe now you could write one final letter to God. Find your pen, open your journal, and write the words that come to you, honest words about your own desire to live radically open to God. Words about what stands in the way. Words about how you want to approach life with God. Words of beseeching, words of consent. Words like *Yes*, and *Please*, and *Let it be so.*

If God were to write back, I wonder what God would say. Don't you?

DIRECTIONS FOR SACRED READING

Read one of the passages of scripture in the Spiritual Exercises slowly and patiently three times with an attitude of openness and receptivity, ready to see whatever it is the Holy Spirit wants to show you.

*First reading—reading with **openness***: As you read the passage the first time, be alert to a word, phrase, or image from this passage that captures your attention. After you finish reading, ponder that word, phrase, or image for a couple of minutes, letting it sink into your heart.

*Second reading—reading with **availability***: Read the passage a second time with this question in mind: How is this passage of scripture connecting with or speaking to my life right now? After you are finished reading, continue to reflect for a couple of minutes on how this passage of scripture is connecting with or speaking to your life right now.

*Third reading—reading with **responsiveness***: Read the passage a third time with this question in mind: Is there an invitation from God for me in this passage, something toward which God is calling me or leading me, or something God is inviting me to do? After you are finished reading, continue to reflect for a couple of minutes on whether there is an invitation from God for you in this passage.

Closing prayer: Close this time of sacred reading by asking God to continue to help you to be open, available, and responsive to God in every aspect of your life and especially to what God has been showing you through this sacred reading of scripture.

NOTES

Introduction: An Invitation

Epigraph. *The American Heritage Dictionary of the English Language*, 4th ed., s.v. "everyday."

1. For more on the practice of spiritual direction see, L. Roger Owens, *Abba, Give Me a Word: The Path of Spiritual Direction* (Brewster, MA: Paraclete, 2012).
2. *The American Heritage Dictionary of the English Language*, 4th ed., s.v. "everyday."
3. Thomas Merton, *New Seeds of Contemplation* (New York: New Directions, 1972), 3.
4. L. Roger Owens, *What We Need Is Here: Practicing the Heart of Christian Spirituality* (Nashville, TN: Upper Room Books, 2015).
5. *The Happiness Lab* [podcast], "Caring What You're Sharing," Erica Boothby interview with Laurie Santos, 25 February 2021, https://www.happinesslab.fm/season-1-episodes/caring-what-youre-sharing.

1. Practicing Spirituality in the Passive Voice: Posture

Epigraph. Augustine, *Confessions*, trans. Henry Chadwick (Oxford: Oxford University Press, 1991), 110.

1. Thomas J. Peters and Robert H. Waterham, Jr. *In Search of Excellence: Lessons from America's Best-Run Companies* (New York: MFJ Books, 2004), 119.
2. Thomas R. Kelly, *A Testament of Devotion* (New York: Harper and Brothers, 1941), 30.
3. Dick Eastman, *The Hour That Changes the World: A Practical Plan for Personal Prayer* (Grand Rapids, MI: Chosen Books, 2002).
4. Charles Spurgeon, quoted in Eastman, *The Hour That Changes the World*, 17.
5. Eastman, *The Hour That Changes the World*, 22.
6. Julian of Norwich, *Revelations of Divine Love*, trans. Elizabeth Spearing (London: Penguin Books, 1998), 101.
7. Richard Foster, *Celebration of Discipline: The Path to Spiritual Growth,* rev. ed. (San Francisco: Harper and Row, 1988), 7.
8. Kyle Cunningham, "Ten Easy Ways to Kill a Tree (And How to Avoid Them)," University of Arkansas Division of Agriculture and Research Extension, https://www.uaex.uada.edu/publications/PDF/FSA-5011.pdf
9. Ruth Burrows, *Essence of Prayer* (New York: HiddenSpring/Paulist, 2006), 28.

2. Following Our Ultimate Desire: Longing

Epigraph. Simon Tugwell, preface to *The Cloud of Unknowing*, ed. James Walsh (New York: Paulist, 1981), xii.

1. James K. A. Smith, *On the Road with Saint Augustine: A Real-World Spirituality for Restless Hearts* (Grand Rapids, MI: Brazos, 2019), 12.
2. J. Brent Bill, *Beauty, Truth, Life, and Love: Four Essentials for the Abundant Life* (Brewster, MA: Paraclete, 2019), 27.
3. Jane E. Vennard, *A Praying Congregation: The Art of Teaching Spiritual Practice* (Herndon, VA: Alban Institute, 2005), 43.
4. Lauren F. Winner, *Still: Notes on a Mid-Faith Crisis* (San Francisco: HarperOne, 2012), 54.

3. Savoring Each Sip of Life: Attention

Epigraph. Wilkie Au, *The Enduring Heart: Spirituality for the Long Haul* (New York: Paulist, 2000), 101.

1. Frederick Buechner, *Now and Then* (San Francisco: HarperSanFrancisco, 1983), 87.
2. Jim Gaffigan, *Food: A Love Story* (New York: Crown Archetype, 2014), 9.
3. Jake Knapp and John Zeratsky, *Make Time: How to Focus on What Matters Everyday* (New York: Crown, 2018), 5.
4. Simone Weil, *Waiting for God* (New York: Harper and Row, 1973), 106.
5. Lauren Winner, review of *Thin Places: Essays from In Between*, by Jordan Kisner, *The Christian Century* (July 15, 2020): 39.
6. Weil, *Waiting for God*, 105.
7. Weil, *Waiting for God*, 106.
8. Weil, *Waiting for God*, 108.
9. Weil, *Waiting for God*, 114.

4. Trading Willfulness for Willingness: Patience

Epigraph. Pierre Teilhard de Chardin, quoted in *Hearts on Fire: Praying with Jesuits*, ed. Michael Harter (St. Louis: The Institute of Jesuit Sources, 1993), 58.

1. Eugene Peterson, *The Contemplative Pastor: Returning to the Art of Spiritual Direction* (Grand Rapids, MI: Eerdmans, 1989), 105–9.
2. Gerald G. May, *Will and Spirit: A Contemplative Psychology* (San Francisco: HarperOne, 1987), 6.
3. May, *Will and Spirit*, 6.
4. May, *Will and Spirit*, 6.
5. Thomas Merton, *New Seeds of Contemplation* (New York: New Directions, 1972), 31.
6. Charles Wesley, "Love Divine, All Loves Excelling," *The United Methodist Hymnal* (Nashville, TN: The United Methodist Publishing House, 1989), 384.
7. Howard Thurman, *Deep Is the Hunger: Meditations for Apostles of Sensitiveness* (New York: Harper and Brothers, 1951), 104.
8. Michael Pollan, *In Defense of Food: An Eater's Manifesto* (New York: Penguin, 2008), 1.

5. Dropping Our Seriousness: Playfulness

Epigraph. Samuel H. Miller, *The Life of the Soul* (New York: Harper and Brothers, 1951), 19.

1. Belden C. Lane, *The Solace of Fierce Landscapes: Exploring Desert and Mountain Spirituality* (New York: Oxford University Press, 1998), 182.

2. Shunryu Suzuki, *Zen Mind, Beginner's Mind* (Boston: Shambhala, 2011), 2.

3. Jon M. Sweeney, *When Saint Francis Saved the Church: How a Converted Medieval Troubadour Created a Spiritual Vision for the Ages* (Notre Dame, IN: Ave Maria Press, 2014), 34.

4. Gerald G. May, *The Dark Night of the Soul: A Psychiatrist Explores the Connection Between Darkness and Spiritual Growth* (San Francisco: HarperOne, 2004), 93.

5. Sweeney, *When Saint Francis Saved the Church*, 25.

6. Sweeney, *When Saint Francis Saved the Church*, 19.

7. Alasdair MacIntyre, *After Virture: A Study in Moral Theology*, 2nd ed. (Notre Dame, IN: University of Notre Dame Press, 1984), 187.

8. For Alasdair MacIntyre's discussion of a practice and his example of chess as one, see *After Virtue*, 187–88.

9. John Chapman, *Spiritual Letters* (New York: Burns and Oates, 2003), 109.

6. Lowering Our Defenses: Vulnerability

Epigraph. Madeleine L'Engle, *Walking on Water: Reflections on Faith and Art* (New York: North Point, 1995), 190.

1. Parker J. Palmer, *Let Your Life Speak: Listening for the Voice of Vocation* (San Francisco: Jossey-Bass, 2000), 7.

2. David Whyte, "Self-Portrait," in *River Flow: New and Selected Poems* (Langley, WA: Many Rivers Press, 2019), 345.

3. John H. Hopkins Jr., "We Three Kings," in *The United Methodist Hymnal* (Nashville, TN: The United Methodist Publishing House, 1989), 254.

4. William C. Placher, *Narratives of a Vulnerable God: Christ, Theology, and Scripture* (Louisville, KY: Westminster John Knox, 1994), 21.

5. Thomas Merton, *New Seeds of Contemplation* (New York: New Directions, 1972), 31.

6. Edward Sellner, "Celtic Soul Friendship and Contemporary Spiritual Mentoring," in *Handbook of Spirituality for Ministry, Volume 2: Perspectives for the 21st Century*, ed. Robert J. Wicks (New York: Paulist Press, 2000), 370.

7. This story about Magaret Guenther was told to me by one of her directees.

8. Placher, *Narratives of a Vulnerable God*, xv.

9. The app I use is called Pray As You Go. https://pray-as-you-go.org/.

7. Saying Goodbye to Goldilocks: Nonjudgment

Epigraph. *The Desert Fathers: Sayings of the Early Christian Monks*, trans. Benedicta Ward (London: Penguin Books, 2003), 85.

1. Thomas Merton, *New Seeds of Contemplation* (New York: New Directions, 1972), 16.

2. Dietrich Bonhoeffer, *Dietrich Bonhoeffer Works*, vol. 5, *Life Together* and *Prayerbook of the Bible*, ed. Geffrey B. Kelly, trans. Daniel W. Bloesch and James H. Burtness (Minneapolis: Fortress Press, 1996), 93.

3. Marjorie Thompson, *Soul Feast*, rev. ed. (Louisville, KY: Westminster John Knox, 2014), 34.

4. Frederick Buechner, *Now and Then* (San Francisco: HarperSanFrancisco, 1991), 87.

5. L. Roger Owens, *What We Need Is Here: Practicing the Heart of Christian Spirituality* (Nashville, TN: Upper Room Books, 2015), 61–64.

6. See John Main, *Essential Writings*, selected and introduced by Laurence Freeman (Maryknoll, NY: Orbis Books, 2002) and Martin Laird, *Into the Silent Land: A Guide to the Christian Practice of Contemplation* (New York: Oxford University Press, 2006).

7. Laird, *Into the Silent Land*, 35.

8. James Finley, *Christian Meditation: Experiencing the Presence of God* (San Francisco: HarperSanFrancisco, 2005), 24.

9. Merton, *New Seeds of Contemplation*, 16.

8. Raising Our Anchors: Freedom

Epigraph. Gerald G. May, *The Dark Night of the Soul: A Psychiatrist Explores the Connection Between Darkness and Spiritual Growth* (San Francisco: HarperOne, 2004), 74.

1. For an account of Ignatius on disordered attachments, see James Martin, SJ, *The Jesuit Guide to (Almost) Everything: A Spirituality for Real Life* (San Francisco: HarperOne, 2010), 180.

2. Thomas Merton, *The New Man* (New York: Farrar, Straus and Giroux, 1961), 101.

3. Rowan Williams, *Where God Happens: Discovering Christ in One Another* (Boston: New Seeds Books, 2005), 95.

4. Martin, *The Jesuit Guide to Almost Everything*, 306–7.

5. *On Being with Krista Tippett* [podcast], "James Martin: Finding God in All Things," interview with James Martin, American Public Media, 1 Dec 2016. https://onbeing.org/programs/james-martin-finding-god-in-all-things-2/.

6. *The Desert Fathers: Sayings of the Early Christian Monks*, trans. Benedicta Ward (London: Penguin Books, 2003), 23.

7. Thomas R. Kelly, *Testament of Devotion* (New York: Harper and Brothers, 1941), 108.

8. Thomas R. Kelly, "Eternal Presence and Temporal Guidance," lecture, box 6, mss. collection no. 1135, Thomas R. Kelly Papers, Haverford College Library, Haverford, PA.

9. Kelly, *Testament of Devotion*, 71–72.

Conclusion

Epigraph. Thomas R. Kelly, *Testament of Devotion* (New York: Harper and Brothers, 1941), 75.

For those who hunger for deep spiritual experience . . .

The Academy for Spiritual Formation® is an experience of disciplined Christian community emphasizing holistic spirituality—nurturing body, mind, and spirit. The program, a ministry of The Upper Room®, is ecumenical in nature and meant for all those who hunger for a deeper relationship with God, including both lay and clergy persons. Each Academy fosters spiritual rhythms—of study and prayer, silence and liturgy, solitude and relationship, rest and play.

With offerings of both Two-Year and Five-Day models, Academy participants rediscover Christianity's rich spiritual heritage through worship, learning, and fellowship. During the Two-Year Academy, pilgrims gather at a retreat center for five days every three months over the course of two years (a total of 40 days), and the Five-Day Academy is a modified version of the Two-Year experience, inviting pilgrims to gather for five days of spiritual learning and worship. The Academy's commitment to an authentic spirituality promotes balance, inner and outer peace, holy living and justice living—God's shalom.

Faculty trained in the wide breadth of Christian spirituality and practice provide content and guidance at each session of The Academy. Academy faculty presenters come from seminaries, monasteries, spiritual direction ministries, and pastoral ministries or other settings and are from a variety of traditions.

The ACADEMY RECOMMENDS program seeks to highlight content that aligns with the Academy's mission to create transformative space for people to connect with God, self, others, and creation for the sake of the world.

Learn more by visiting academy.upperroom.org.